One
Woman
Against
the Reich

One Woman Against the Reich

Helmut W. Ziefle with Glenn F. Arnold

25209

BETHANY ⧫ HOUSE PUBLISHERS
Minneapolis, Minnesota 55438
A Division of Bethany Fellowship, Inc.

The people, places and incidents in this story are all real. However, the names of certain individuals have been changed in the interest of privacy.

Published by Bethany House Publishers
Division of Bethany Fellowship, Inc.
6820 Auto Club Road, Minneapolis, Minnesota 55438

Printed in the United States of America

Library of Congress Catologing in Publication Data

Ziefle, Helmut W., 1939-
  One woman against the Reich.

  1. Ziefle, Maria. 2. Ziefle family.
3. Anti-Nazi movement—Germany (West)—Heilbronn. 4. Sontheim (Heilbronn, Germany)—Biography. 5. Heilbronn (Germany)—Biography. 6. Christian biography—Germany (West)—Heilbronn. I. Arnold, Glenn F., 1933-
II. Title.
DD901.S654Z538   943'.46 [B]   81-7721
ISBN 0-87123-414-9   AACR2

DEDICATION

To my parents, who taught me by their lives the meaning of
Christian discipleship.

ACKNOWLEDGMENTS

I have received invaluable help from two sources. The first is my brother, Kurt. Being twelve years my senior, he remembers many more of the incidents which are recounted in this book. I greatly appreciate his additions and corrections.

Secondly, I received much useful technical information about the air attacks on Heilbronn from the book *Heilbronn—Die schwersten Stunden der Stadt*, by Wilhelm Steinhilber (Stadt Heilbronn, Stadtarchiv, 1961).

Thanks to these and other sources, the historical accuracy of this story has been verified.

FOREWORD

Many books have been written on the Holocaust and on what it meant to live during the years when Hitler came to power. All of these books offer powerful insight into the horrors of a monstrous political and genocidal machine that crept up on an unwary population and literally decimated it within a few short years.

This book, however, recounts that era through the eyes of a *Christian* family. The world has had many long looks at what the Jews suffered; but few, if any, have understood what the Christian had to face, especially when children were caught between the glory of the Hitler youth movement and the biblical drumbeat that became muted amidst the panorama of swastikas and "Brown Shirts."

This book is of extreme significance to Christians—and to anyone for that matter—who must consider how any political ideology can control, to the extent of ripping families apart and estranging their members to the point of hostility and enmity.

The writers have focused sharply on the pain and confusion that the faithful must endure in a totalitarian society. The authors also have carefully pointed out that even those in the faith can bend under this burden. From carefully wrought details and the broader strokes of the Nazi tidal wave that seemed destined to engulf the Ziefle family, there emerges a chronicle that should cause the comfortable American Christian to take time for serious consideration regarding the waves of history that continue to roll along.

The book also reveals the courage of believers facing the

crush of political dominance which produces the gold of God that comes with suffering. If such suffering is someday to be the lot of the American Christian family, and who really knows how soon, then this book will provide excellent preparation for such a time.

Above all, this book shows that God is never far outside the events that surround us and is ever able and willing to affect those events to save His own. Here is a book that is disturbing but also inspiring and deserves the attention of Christians everywhere.

James L. Johnson,
Co-ordinator, Journalism Dept.
Wheaton College Graduate School

INTRODUCTION

The 1976 Bicentennial celebration of the United States' independence was a magnificent tribute to the hopes and aspirations of free men everywhere. In the five years following, the nation has been increasingly confronted with serious domestic and foreign challenges which mock the people who have viewed themselves as champions of freedom and justice.

These challenges are calling for "instant" opportunistic solutions which ridicule the time-tested heritage of biblical morality. Exchanging scriptural principles for more "pragmatic" answers will only lead to a dismal end. Hitler attempted this when he tantalized German society with promises of millennial Aryan supremacy. The eventual humiliation and destruction of Nazi Germany bear grim testimony to the end of such philosophies.

Hitler's demands for total allegiance and the sacrifice of individual freedom were a direct affront to those who were already submitted to the lordship of Jesus Christ. The German Christians whose spiritual senses had been honed sharp by their walk with God were not fooled by the Führer's impossible promises. And they suffered for their faith. No one, of course, suffered under Hitler more than the Jews; but the Gentile followers of the Messiah were also an oppressed minority.

This book contains the story of one such family—mine. Until I was six years old, I did not know of peace except at home, where God's peace reigned. To stand up for truth was costly—especially for my parents. Truth has never been a cheap commodity.

There is no promise that the incidents in this book could not someday take place in the United States. All that would be required is a deluded leader with convincing promises. Unfortunately, it seems that the country is ripe for such a phenomenon.

I am an American citizen by choice, not by birth. I treasure the freedoms this nation affords. Yet they can easily be lost if God's people do not speak loudly and pray urgently against the immoral trends in our society. I pray that this book will help to awaken and inspire you to do just that.

Helmut W. Ziefle

I
Autumn 1938

*In my Teutonic order, a youth will grow up which
will frighten the world. I want a fierce, masterful,
fearless and ferocious youth. It can't show any weakness or tenderness. The free and magnificent beast of
prey must finally glow again from their eyes.*

—Adolf Hitler

The gold of autumn was magic to the German spirit.
Gilded forests and mountains and the brisk air of southern
Germany intoxicated its people with exuberance. Undaunted by the impending struggle with winter, man and woman
embraced life with renewed determination.

But Maria Ziefle lay silent and tense in the darkened
bedroom, her eyes staring at the ceiling, sleep evading her.

*In the chill of the midnight, as I lie warm with my mate,
I feel cold that creeps into my soul—a death, a poison that
few speak of, even if asked. There are sounds in the distance. First the clapping of hands, then the stamping of feet
accompanying male voices in songs of German pride and
might. The steady beating of boots upon our cobblestone
street is the worst. I shiver.*

*The tentacles of the swastika are enclosing even little
Sontheim. God, I am afraid—for my family, for my
country. I am helpless; my husband is helpless; and my
three children, most of all. God, give us grace and strength
for whatever we must endure.*

Shaking off her weariness from the sleepless night, Maria proceeded with her domestic routines—a morning trip to the butcher, the bakery, and finally the food market just around the corner. In the afternoon she beat the living-room rug, washed bedding, and put a roast in the oven. In Heilbronn's gentle suburb of Sontheim, life still appeared ordinary.

Maria paused before the mirror in the upstairs corridor. Smoothing her brown hair back into the little bun at the nape of her neck, she stepped closer to check her work and hesitated. The blue eyes seemed faded, her full cheeks had lost their lively ruddiness; her face was now drawn and lined. The gray dress only accentuated her aged appearance. This Nazi thing was wearing at her soul. But supper had to be cooked.

As she turned away with a sigh and began descending the stairs, the front door banged shut and footsteps clattered in the hall.

"Mama!" Eleven-year-old Kurt exclaimed, breathless as he halted at the bottom of the steps. Maria couldn't help but smile at her second son's exuberance. Dark blond, athletic and adventurous, he was the near fulfillment of the Aryan dream. But no national dream could account for the joy this son brought to a mother's heart.

"Mama, I joined the Jungvolk[1] today! The meeting was terrific!" He paused expectantly, his bright face upturned toward Maria.

Halfway down the steps, Maria's smile faded as she stared at her second child. His dancing brown eyes and flushed innocence were untarnished; but the poison was now in her home.

"Aren't you happy I joined?" he asked finally.

Her throat tightened, but she pushed the words out stiffly. "Son, do you forget so easily?"

---

1. The Young Folk, the junior division (ages 10-14) of the Hitler Youth organization.

"What do you mean, Mama?" He looked puzzled.

"No matter what you join"— her voice had regained its steady confidence—"remember that first, you belong to Jesus."

Maria and George Ziefle had carefully nurtured their three children's impressionable spirits. Reinhold, the oldest and now 13, Kurt, and ten-year-old Ruth were the objects of their parents' frequent prayers and regular Bible teaching. The Creator and His written Word wielded unquestioned authority in the Ziefle household.

But the trusting minds of German children were now subject to strong, more adamant voices. Men were extolling a new plan to restore the nation's shaken glory. For five years the militarism of the "new liberation" movement had been propagated through radio, films, parades and rallies. The voices spoke of a superior race, heroism for the fatherland, and allegiance to the Führer. And God was pushed aside as a pathetic bystander.

Three years earlier, Julius Streicher, founder of *Der Stürmer*[2], told 200,000 youth at a festival on Hesenberg Mountain that Jesus Christ was "the greatest anti-Semite of all time." Urging them toward a united hatred of Jews, he warned, "Don't believe in priests as long as they defend people whom Christ called 'sons of the devil.' "

Such group pressure was strong for a pre-adolescent like Kurt. The disciplines, the parades, and the camaraderie appealed to him. And the God-cemented foundations of his life had not yet cured. When Hitler visited Heilbronn in 1934, Kurt had eagerly gone, against his parents' wishes, to watch the Führer's motorcade. Because he was just a child, he was allowed to stand at the front of the crowd. The thrill of saluting the Aryan "messiah" with thousands of other bystanders left a strong impression on his mind. Innocently he had embraced the hopes of Naziism.

Maria's supper preparations were more from habit

---

2. *The Stormer*, a Nazi newspaper.

than concentration that evening. The five Ziefles eagerly gathered for the meal as lukewarm rays of autumn sunset illuminated the dining room of their beige stucco house. Kurt, pulling himself and his chair closer to the steaming beef roast, announced above the conversation, "From now on, we must all greet one another by saying, 'Heil Hitler!' "

The happy chatter ceased; silence gripped them as if it were a strangler. Four pairs of eyes turned toward Maria.

Her lips tightened as she glanced downward to avoid the pleading stares. "No, Kurt." Her voice was resolute. Maria lifted her eyes toward him and swallowed. "We do not salute a man in place of God. In this house we will continue to say, 'Grüss Gott.'[3] Is that understood?"

"Yes, Mama." He hung his head, trying to hide his embarrassment. George nodded his approval, and a smile of admiration showed beneath his dark mustache. A man of modest physique, he was unmatched in his aggressive selling of sewing machines for the Singer Company of Heilbronn. Both friends and business colleagues respected his keen balance of ambition and high moral standards, and his success had provided his family with a comfortable life. For spiritual wisdom, however, he often looked to his wife, who humbly received a flow of authoritative insight from the Lord whom they both followed.

Supper, though subdued, continued without further incident. Maria cleaned the kitchen, then finished the hem on a new skirt for Ruth. The children worked on school assignments and George finished his newspaper. Bedtime was approaching, but first there must be "Dämmerstündle."

The devotional time at dusk had been a ten-year tradition in this household. Centuries before, Martin Luther had stressed the importance of family togetherness and Christian education of children in the home; George and Maria accepted it as a divine commission.

Maria called the children to the second-story living

---

3. "May God greet you."

room, the three crowding together onto the couch. Their parents each pulled up a chair facing them. Except for the dancing glow from the coal stove, the room was in darkness.

Maria began with a story from the Bible, told in her own inimitable way. The truths regarding the Almighty came easily to her, and no theologian could make men and women of Scripture seem more exciting and alive. The family joined in singing several hymns and choruses, Ruth accompanying them on the pump organ that stood in the corner of the room with Kurt playing his violin. Then, in their own darkened sanctuary, they knelt on the floor and each, in turn, prayed.

As was her custom, Maria concluded with a German story of moral courage, of which she seemed to know dozens. This was her way of applying biblical truths to everyday life. The stories delighted the children and they would beg her to retell them again and again.

After Reinhold, Kurt and Ruth proceeded to their beds, Maria and George silently descended the stairway and entered their bedroom on the first floor. As her husband closed the door behind them, Maria slipped both arms around his waist and pulled him close to her. Alone with him in the darkness, her eyes glistened with moisture and her lips trembled. "I'm afraid of the future," she began, her voice quivering. "I know that if we bring our problem to the Lord, He will work it out—but how? How can we save our children? Now Reinhold and Kurt are required to attend meetings where they are taught to hate God, the Church— even Jews. And the Nazis make it so difficult for people who won't cooperate with them."

George stepped away for a moment to close the shutters. He shivered from the autumn coolness—and from that strange chill which seemed to thrive in the darkness. He returned and kissed his wife.

He spoke softly to avoid disturbing Ruth in the adjoining room. "For thirteen years of marriage I've devoted all my strength to providing for and protecting our family. I'm so proud of our sons and our daughter. I'll do anything to insure that they follow our Savior." As they prepared for bed he continued, "For now, we will have to let them attend the meetings—that is the law. But that is no problem for the Lord, is it? With His help, we will preserve them. I'm sure I pray ten times a day, 'God, keep Reinhold, Kurt and Ruth from being destroyed by the Nazi philosophies.' "

The couple climbed into bed and pulled the comforter over them. Maria slid close and whispered, "If only more men in Germany prayed for their children as you do, this Nazi thing would never have begun."

"I don't think that I've done anything very great, but I know how important *your* influence is in our family. You are a good wife and mother, Maria, and your faith in the Lord has been rewarded with wonderful children who love you." George stopped for a moment. "I don't like to be negative about my country; I love Germany very much. But you and I both realize that there are bad things going on. Yet, I think that whatever happens to the nation, God can keep our family. Don't you agree?"

Maria replied slowly, "I don't feel very confident about it, but I know you're right. God has never let us down."

"No use lying here worrying, then," George said with a comforting squeeze. "Let's get some rest." He kissed his wife heartily, then rolled over and fell asleep almost instantly.

Why can't I fall asleep so easily? God, I do trust that you will take good care of us. But the future is so uncertain. What will happen to us, to our children? I would not want them to face the hardships I faced as a child.

Thoughts of her early years raced through Maria's consciousness. Her mother had died when Maria was nine. A year later, her father remarried, but his new wife resented the stepchildren. Often she sent them to school without breakfast, and during the winter she shut them out of the heated portion of the house.

At 15, Maria escaped from the oppressive homelife and

obtained work as a housekeeper in Stuttgart. Not only did she gain relief from her spiteful stepmother, but she learned strict standards of housekeeping and became an accomplished seamstress. These were skills she put to good use in her own home. And she never forgot the misery of living in a home without love.

You've filled my heart with love for my children, Heavenly Father. Don't let our family be torn apart by this Nazi regime. Keep our faith from wavering, whatever comes.

Sewing machine sales had been very brisk that week, so George took Friday afternoon off to do some errands. "I'll be back in an hour, Mama," he called to his wife as he buttoned his jacket. Pulling the front door shut behind him, he walked past the small flower bed and climbed onto his bicycle; he was riding to the Woolworth store in Heilbronn to purchase school supplies for the children.

Concern gripped Maria's heart as she ran from the kitchen and flung open the door. "Be careful! Too many strange things have been happening in the streets," she called in warning as George pedaled out the gate.

He disappeared beyond the fence, but she could hear him from the street. "Don't worry, Mama, I'll watch out."

Jews in the Heilbronn area had been increasingly harassed by the Nazis during the previous months. Even the Ziefles' physician, Dr. Picard, had been receiving threatening phone calls. Now there was talk that Nazi "Brown Shirts" had been slashing tires of bicycles parked in front of Jewish-owned stores, including Woolworth's. George dismissed it as mere rumor.

As he pedaled down the street, George warmly greeted neighbors and business acquaintances. After fifteen minutes, he was parking his bicycle among a dozen others in front of Woolworth's.

The door banged loudly behind him when George reentered the house. Maria glanced up as he stamped into the kitchen. His face taut with rage, he slammed his fist on the counter.

"I was in the Woolworth store only ten minutes—ten minutes! And when I came out, those thugs had slit both of my tires open!"

"Where is your bicycle now?" Maria's voice trembled slightly.

"I had to push it all the way home. Maria, this matter is going too far. If these barbarians aren't stopped, they'll soon be doing even worse things to Jews in our town. God won't tolerate the persecution of innocent people!"

"Papa, why don't we pray right now for our Jewish friends—and our children." They knelt together by the couch.

As the couple rose from their knees several minutes later, their faith renewed, Reinhold and Kurt dashed into the house, their bags thumping against their legs.

"How was school today, boys?" their father greeted them with a smile. He hoped that they had not left their sister too far behind as they ran.

The boys looked at each other, hesitating. "We won't be having religious instruction any more. They've changed it to 'Weltanschauungsunterricht.' "[4]

"Who's teaching the class?" George asked flatly.

"Oh, we still have the same teacher—Director Otterbacher."

The parents smiled with relief as Kurt told them, "Today he told us about the greatness of the twelve tribes of Israel." Kurt was not very enthusiastic about religious subjects, but he admired Otterbacher for continuing his excellent Bible teaching in the face of harassment.

Even at 11, Kurt was very perceptive of a man's character. He had little respect for men who abandoned their principles out of fear, as his grade-school teacher, Herr Weber, had done. Weber originally professed to be a Christian, but

---

4. Instruction in Nazi philosophy.

when the Nazis rose to power, he quickly succumbed to their philosophies and taught them in the school.

Kurt, recognizing the character differences between such men, continued to respect the Bible teacher. George and Maria were confident that as long as Otterbacher taught, their boys would receive sound Christian instruction; he would not give in to the demands of the Nazis.

Sunday was approaching, bringing with it another crisis for the Ziefle parents. Up until this time, school hours had been set aside each Wednesday for Nazi indoctrination and paramilitary drills. But beginning that month, attendance would also be required at Jungvolk rallies on the second Sunday of each month. On October 8, Reinhold and Kurt would be expected to miss church and attend the rally.

Conversation at the breakfast table that Sunday was subdued. Each person seemed to sense that conflict hovered over them. As she was clearing the table, Maria saw Kurt approach solemnly. Her heart sank as he said, "Mother, you know that I must go to Jungvolk this morning. I'll be back in time for lunch." He turned and headed for the doorway.

Maria turned slowly toward Reinhold. "Are you going to go with him?"

"No, Mama. I'm a Christian, and I'm going to church."

Her erect German spirit barely restrained the tears and the embrace that she longed to give him. "That is good, Son. That is good."

The four Ziefles walked quietly out the gate and down Ackermannstrasse. Dwarfed by the huge red brick Ackermann yarn factories lining both sides of the street, Reinhold and Ruth strolled together wearing the new navy blue outfits their mother had made. Maria was absorbed in thoughts about the missing member of their family.

In ten minutes they had reached the only Protestant church in Sontheim. As they approached the steps of the Matthäuskirche on Hauptstrasse, "Brown Shirts" and

Nazi sympathizers had gathered in front of their head-quarters across the street to heckle the faithful. Loudly some of them threatened to pelt the churchgoers with chunks of wood. The Ziefles mounted the steps silently, looking straight ahead.

Inside, the sanctuary seemed painfully barren. Church attendance was discouraged by the Nazi regime. Of the congregation's 2,000 members, only about 20 were present this morning—mostly older women. Even the beautiful ceiling fresco of Christ as the Lamb of God appeared stark and cold in the nearly empty building.

At 10:30 the bell was rung and Pastor Brendle approached the lectern. He offered a short invocation, then announced the hymn, "Praise to the Lord, the Almighty, the King of Creation." The voices of the meager congregation, without organ accompaniment, echoed weakly from the walls of the large edifice.

As she sang, Maria gazed with concern at the pastor. His muscular shoulders drooped as if he were much older than his forty years. His hair seemed thinner, and his eyes—sadness and frustrated concern had left their shadows.

Three years earlier, in response to the Nazis' tighter controls on churches, he criticized their betrayal of the non-intervention policy in an article in the church bulletin. He had quoted Paul in Galatians: " . . . false brethren unawares brought in, who came in privily to spy out our liberty which we have in Christ Jesus, that they might bring us into bondage." The Nazis retaliated by banning his bulletin for about six months.

Unable to criticize the government from his pulpit lest he be arrested, Brendle nonetheless did all he could to insure the spiritual welfare of his parishioners. He persistently fought to uphold the use of Scripture and religious instruction. The Gestapo kept him under close scrutiny, and school officials continually criticized him. At one point the Nazis even closed the church and prevented Brendle from giving religious instruction in the school, on the pretext of a foot-and-mouth disease in the area. This harassment was a brazen affront to German law and tradition.

As the hymn drew to a close, the blare of trumpets and raucous voices singing Hitler's songs savagely invaded the quiet sanctuary. Pastor Brendle self-consciously climbed up to the pulpit for the sermon. After an uncertain moment he began to preach, but could hardly be heard.

George leaped from the pew, his face red with anger. Maria desperately grasped the tail of his coat and pulled him down to his seat.

"Don't do anything now," she whispered urgently, "for our family's sake—and the church's." Her fingers still clutched his woolen jacket. His hands trembling and jaw clenched, George remained in the seat.

The pastor dutifully continued with his sermon, though he could barely hear himself above the loud songs and shouts outside the windows. His unflinching self-control was the greatest sermon he had delivered in months. Frequent oral treatises on complex orthodoxies only bewildered his flock. Today their shepherd's message reached their hearts, though hardly a word was audible.

Ruth's merrily swinging braids did little to lighten the Ziefles' solemnity as they walked home. Their feelings needed little discussion. Even Maria's emotional control was visibly shaken.

As their children walked on ahead, George growled in a low voice, "When will it end, Mama? My patience is nearly gone. There's been so much tension at work, in our home, and now—in church!"

"I wish I had an answer." Maria's eyes gazed far ahead. "God knows. But somehow that really doesn't seem enough, does it?"

Kurt was waiting for the family at the gate when they arrived home. Beaming, he exclaimed, "Let me tell you what we did at Jungvolk this morning!" The family silently walked toward the front door.

II
October 1938

Adolf Hitler! We are united with you alone! On this earth we believe in Adolf Hitler alone. We believe that National Socialism is the sole redeeming faith for our nation.

—Dr.Robert Ley (head of the National
Socialist Labor Front)

Maria restrained her determined stride as she approached the Neckar River which angled across the northern edge of Sontheim. Here she could slow her pace after a busy morning of errands and housework. The ground was mottled with fallen leaves, and early afternoon sunlight danced warmly through the half-barren tree branches. She inhaled deeply in the crisp breeze that blew over the river. This was a welcome respite from the crowded neighborhood and necessary therapy for her phlebitis.

But these regular walks were, more importantly, a time for communion with her Lord, a sacred hour to muse upon scripture she had carefully read as she ate her lunch of soup and bread. And now there was so much to consider and to tell to her Master; at forty years of age, Maria was once again pregnant.

"Well, Frau Ziefle, you were right," Dr. Picard had announced with a grin across his usually serious face; "you are going to have a baby. Probably in early April, before the time you Christians call Easter—Passover to us, of course."

"I don't know how George is going to take this," replied Maria slowly, as she stared out the window of the office. "In fact, I almost wish for the child's sake that this baby wouldn't have to be born. These are not pleasant times for a little one to enter the world."

"But life is never easy, is it?"

"Do you know, Doctor, that I have dreamed three times in the last month that I was giving birth to a child? Each time I seemed to hear the voice of God assuring me that all would be well, and the child would be protected. And I'm sure it was God speaking to me."

"Your faith amazes me, Frau Ziefle. You realize there can be complications for a pregnant woman of your age? But you are strong and healthy, aside from your phlebitis, and with such faith, who knows, maybe you will give birth to an Isaac! His mother was 90, you know."

"I know, Doctor."

In spite of Maria's misgivings, George had shown almost boyish delight at the prospect of another child. For him it was a happy diversion from the mounting pressures that seemed to touch every aspect of their lives. George's excitement greatly eased the burden on Maria's mind.

Also prominent in her thoughts this afternoon was the coming weekend. Maria had recently written a letter to her sister and brother-in-law, Berta and Christian Haier of Maubach, asking if the Ziefles could spend Friday and Saturday night at their home. The reply had not yet come. The family needed to get away. The pressure of the threats and angry looks of the Nazis was slowly mounting, and a weekend retreat from their surroundings would give George and Maria a chance to untangle their thoughts.

Lord, we need that reply from Berta. It's such a small thing for you to hurry a letter through the mails. We need to breathe the peaceful air of Maubach, to be assured that you are the God who gives peace. You have promised so clearly that you will take care of this baby inside me. Please, give me the same hope for the rest of my family.

Maria's concentration turned to the traffic on Kolping-strasse while she attempted to cross the busy thoroughfare. As she reached the other side and entered Ackermann-strasse, a sense of something strong and bright surged within her. Her spirit responded to the Presence, and for a moment her steps seemed lighter and her shoulders straightened with youthful vigor.

"Heil Hitler!"

Maria turned her head to see Herr Müller, her neighbor, approaching on his bicycle. She nodded and smiled. The man slowly dropped his salute and wagged his head disapprovingly. The neighbors had been increasingly insistent that the Ziefles salute in the Führer's name. Müller would probably report the incident to Herr Schmidt, the highest-ranking Nazi in the neighborhood. Maria resolutely put the incident out of her mind.

As she entered the gate in front of the house, Maria optimistically ran toward the brown steel mailbox by the door. She flipped the top open and slipped her fingers in. There was an envelope. Her heart pounding, she jerked it out and gave the handwriting a quick glance; it was Berta's irregular script!

She hurried through the doorway and up the stairs, tearing the envelope open as she went. Maria eagerly settled herself on the couch in the living room to read:

Dear Maria,

    I was so happy to hear from you again! I agree that these are troublesome times, but things are much quieter in Maubach, I'm sure. Christian was wondering yesterday when we would be able to visit with you and George again. We will look forward to seeing you Friday night when. . . .

Maria stopped and shut damp eyes. Words were not necessary. Her heart expressed to the heavens all the appreciation she felt. That brightness surged afresh in her.

On Friday, Maria hurried through her housekeeping duties in order to prepare for the weekend trip. She wanted to bake a cake after lunch, and also pack the suitcase so that the family would not be delayed in leaving. By foregoing her afternoon stroll, she finished the baking and had time for a short nap before the children arrived—carrying a child at her age was taxing her energy.

As the three young Ziefles returned, Maria laid a large brown suitcase on her bed and called to them, "Children, change out of your school clothes. As soon as you're finished, bring the outfits you will wear to church on Sunday so I can pack them."

One by one they delivered their clothes to her bedroom. As they arrived, Maria assigned each a job: "Ruth, peel the potatoes for supper; Reinhold, run to the fabric shop to purchase the sewing notions which Berta requested; and, Kurt (with some convincing), clean the ashes from the heating stove, the oven in the kitchen, and the water boiler in the laundry."

When George arrived from work, the potatoes and sausage were boiling and the suitcase was ready. The five ate more quickly than usual, for they all wanted to leave for Maubach as early as possible. As soon as they finished eating, each carried the dishes into the kitchen. Maria and Ruth washed them while George prepared the car and Reinhold and Kurt ran to Krauters', who shared the north half of Ziefles' cellar, and asked them to watch the house.

Eagerly the three children clambered into the back seat of their green BMW automobile. Since there was poor train service to Maubach, the family always traveled there by car. They had not seen their aunt and uncle since March when they left Sontheim to avoid the Austria annexation referendum. Maubach was always one of their favorite places to visit. The sun was a bright ball, low in the west, as their vehicle droned past the last scattered houses of Sontheim. There were only 30 miles between Sontheim and Maubach, so no one settled down very much.

"I'm going to help Uncle Christian in his blacksmith shop tomorrow," Reinhold declared.

"You can work in that smelly old place if you want to," Kurt retorted, "but I'm going to play with Waldi." Waldi was a bushy, black-haired mongrel whom the children adored.

"Mama, why can't we have a dog, too?" Ruth asked as usual when the subject of Waldi arose.

Maria smiled and shook her head. "Where would we keep one? Our yard is so small, we hardly have space for our little garden."

"But we could get a little Dachshund and keep him in the house," suggested Kurt.

"Oh, no. No puppies in the house—but I tell you what. I think we may be able to have a little surprise in the spring!" Maria and George glanced at each other, trying to contain their amusement.

"Do you mean a pet, Mama?" Ruth almost jumped over the front seat in her excitement.

"Well, you *might* call it that," Maria answered thoughtfully.

"A cat!" exclaimed Kurt. "But if it's as lazy as Krauters' old Erhardt, I don't want it."

"Oh, it's much nicer than a cat—and more useful too." Maria was enjoying the guessing game, and George chuckled quietly as he drove.

"Is it a rabbit?" Reinhold joined in the game, also puzzled. "Or maybe a chicken?"

"A chicken?" Ruth looked at him with her nose wrinkled up. "What kind of pet is that?"

"I know," George interrupted. He patted his wife's knee to assure her he wasn't about to spill her secret. "I bet it's a piggy! What could be more useful than that? And your mother said it would be a surprise."

The children glanced at each other and shrugged their shoulders in bewilderment. Reinhold quipped, "I'll bet we'll be the only family in Sontheim with a piggy for a pet!"

They all laughed and began to discuss names for their future "piggy."

The Ziefles arrived at Maubach in less than an hour. Eager to start their activities early—their cousins, Gerhard and Hans, would have a full day planned—the children went to bed quickly. The adults were then free to discuss their concerns over the troubles rising around them. It was best not to bring up such subjects in front of the young ones, for one of them might innocently quote a parent's opinions to a schoolteacher or neighbor—a dangerous mistake.

The midnight tramping of boots and the harassment of good people by "Brown Shirts" had not yet infected Maubach. Though George and Maria were not about to ignore their troubles, the two days away from Sontheim were a happy retreat from their daily anxieties. The warm greetings between neighbors and the tranquil orderliness of well-kept farmland invigorated their fatigued souls.

As the Ziefles awakened Saturday morning, they savored the gentle sounds of this rural village. Sontheim's early-morning rumbling from the Ackermann mill and the bustling traffic on Kolpingstrasse were out of sight and sound. Rather, one's ears were soothed by the pastoral chorus of restless milk cows awaiting the farmer and his pail, feasting pigs, and egostistical roosters.

The hard-working country folk enjoyed variety and substance at the dinner table, qualities that were only a distant memory to their city cousins. And their conversations acknowledged a disdain of fretful business pursuits and a delight with life—they spoke of neighbors and friends and the earth which sustained them.

The Ziefle children worked and played with their cousins, relishing in the simple delights of searching for the hens' eggs and kicking a soccer ball down the little-used streets. George enjoyed the release of physical work as he assisted Christian in the blacksmith shop. Maria basked in the warm gentleness of caring for the livestock with Berta.

The contented grunting of the pigs and the gentle clucking of the hens helped to soothe Maria's tense mind. She mused over her predicament.

Why can't we be blessed with such a happy place to live, Lord? Here people love and trust each other. We have a nice house and a car, but the people of Maubach are rich in kindness. Whatever happens around us in Sontheim, please keep love in our family.

A highlight of the weekend was the time of concerned prayer with Berta and Christian on Saturday night. It helped to dissipate George and Maria's sense of aloneness which had almost overwhelmed them in the preceding weeks.

As the Haiers and the Ziefles walked to the church on Sunday morning, they were joined on the street by many other families. It seemed strange to the Ziefles not to be alone in the pursuit of spiritual fellowship and worship. As they neared the building, Maria tensed, then forced herself to relax. She smiled at herself—there were no "Brown Shirts" here.

The church building, both inside and out, was simple. So were the people and their pastor. Their singing was unrefined but vigorous. The sermon was understandable; the God of this pastor seemed much more accessible, much more personal, than their own pastor's God. George and Maria were heartened by the assurance that there was still love and faith in Germany.

The rest of the day progressed all too quickly. Not wanting to return home late, George, Maria, and the children ate an early supper with their relatives and headed for Sontheim before six o'clock. They reached their home as the sunset was fading, but with their optimism rekindled. There seemed to be no insurmountable problems on the horizon.

As if the weekend had been some kind of magical potion, the next few days were unusually placid; Kurt talked little of the Jungvolk meeting, the neighbors seemed more cordial, and George's sales were exceptional. Even Maria began to think that maybe life was on the swing back toward normal.

But the pendulum swung back viciously on the following Friday afternoon. Maria was in the kitchen cheerfully ironing George's pants when she heard the clatter of shoes on the tile of the foyer below. She stepped through the living room toward the stairway and caught a glimpse of the clock on the china closet—two-thirty. *Much too early for the children,* she thought.

"Maria!" A woman's frenzied scream rang up the steps. "Maria, they've taken Wilhelm!"

Maria rushed into the corridor just as her sister-in-law, Paula Glaser, came stumbling to the top of the stairs, shrieking hysterically. Maria ran toward Paula, her arms outstretched. The woman collapsed against her, sobbing fitfully.

Holding her firmly, Maria led her into the living room and gently sat her in a chair at the large wooden table. She pulled the adjoining chair closer and held the woman's head on her shoulder, stroking her dark brown hair. Paula's entire body convulsed with each sob. After a few minutes, Paula began to quiet down.

"Who has taken Wilhelm—and where?" Maria questioned between Paula's sobs.

"The Gestapo"—her speech was broken by rhythmic, jerky whimpers—"committed him to Weissenhof, the mental hospital."

"Weissenhof? Wilhelm is not insane! There must be some mistake."

"A Nazi official came to my door just before noon, Maria, and told me. He claimed Wilhelm had suddenly gone mad. I told him that was impossible."

Paula continued, but her sobbing increased. "He looked at me as if I were some child and said, 'Frau, you are wrong. Your husband called Hitler a scoundrel in front of several other workers. We had no choice but to consider him insane.' " She laid her face on the table and wept helplessly. Maria waited quietly; instinctively her thoughts turned to the Almighty.

Why do you allow the good men to suffer? Why do the godless rule our land? Am I supposed to walk into Hitler's office and slap his hands? God, you must stop this horror— only you can. If you do not stop this, we may all die.

Her lips rigidly pressed together, her own eyes filled with tears. Inwardly, Maria screamed, *I'm helpless, Lord! I'm just one woman against the Reich!* She calmed herself. *I should have known that this week was too good to be true. But how was I to expect something like this? My own brother behind bars!*

Paula began to regain control. Maria cradled the quivering hands in her own, blinked away her own tears and looked directly into the tear-stained face. "Did you go to the Kupfer-Asbest[5] factory to find out what really happened?"

"I went right away. I found Wilhelm's foreman, but he seemed hardly bothered by the matter. He confirmed that Wilhelm had called Hitler a scoundrel. As soon as Wilhelm said it, the foreman called the Gestapo; they came and wrestled him to the floor and took him away to the hospital.

"Then—and I've never heard anyone speak so coldly— he sneered, 'Everyone must be sacrificed for the Party. You should be glad you're rid of that traitor. He's lucky he's still alive.' Right after that, I came straight here."

Maria thought of her childhood when she and her brothers and sisters lived under the oppression of their stepmother. She remembered the cold winter nights in their home near the Black Forest, and how she piled blankets on Wilhelm and the others to keep them warm. He was now 36, but she knew that he needed her just as much now as when he was only 5.

"We have to see him; that's the first thing we must do," Maria began matter-of-factly, trying to contrive a plan as

---

5. Copper-Asbestos.

she spoke. Her face brightened. "That's it! We'll go through Doctor Wagner. He's a high official in the Nazi Party; George knows him very well. I'm sure he will help us."

"Maria, I'm so glad I have you to help me." Paula's reddened eyes glimmered with fresh hope.

"Don't lean on me, Paula. Lean on God. He is the only one who will never fail—even if our circumstances seem hopeless. And right now, I don't know how even He can get us out of this mess. But He will."

Paula nodded meekly.

When George arrived home and received the news, he sat in stunned silence. The mounting inhumanities of the local Nazis continually angered him, but suddenly it had all become very personal. He and Wilhelm had been good friends. He paced about the living room, shaking his fists and muttering, "Animals! Germany is being governed by animals!"

Paula gladly accepted the Ziefles' invitation to spend the night. Dämmerstündle, especially, would be a great encouragement to her. There was also another guest for the devotional time that evening—Otto Steiner, the local baker's journeyman. Of late he had become a frequent visitor at the late evening event, always giving a jaunty knock at the door and entering without waiting for an answer.

Otto was Catholic; and through his contacts at the bakery with Maria and his eventual visits to the home, he had embraced Christ as his own Lord. Now he enjoyed the opportunity to fellowship with the Ziefles; and Otto would pray with them and take his turn reading aloud from the Bible George had given him. He seemed to look on Maria as a second mother, and she enjoyed the opportunity to give him advice and pray for him.

As they prayed for Wilhelm that night, they also voiced their concerns for their nation. None of them wanted to see Germany fall into moral decay.

The next day, George visited Dr. Wagner at his office and asked him to secure permission for them to visit Wilhelm. Wagner, longtime business acquaintance of George's, was happy to oblige. By the next Friday, George, Maria, and Paula received clearance to go to Weissenhof.

The scene at the hospital was beyond their imaginations. Wilhelm had become a slobbering, grunting, writhing madman. He did not even recognize his wife. The three stared in horror through the bars of the cell. Finally Paula broke the silence, no longer able to stifle her wails. The woman's knees began to falter, so Maria and George grabbed her arms and led her to a nearby chair.

"Take me home," she whispered through white lips. Her eyes stared blankly. "It's hopeless; there's nothing I can do for him now." She held her head, a long wail again escaping her.

George and Maria stared at each other in bewilderment. Maria motioned for him to join her a few feet down the corridor from Paula. "Papa, something tells me that things are not as they seem," Maria whispered. "I think they have done something to Wilhelm to make him seem crazy. He has been too stable a man to suddenly act like this."

"I felt the same way as soon as I saw him. If Wilhelm were insane now, we'd have noticed some warning signs before this. I'll see if Wagner can get me some answers."

George made several telephone calls to Dr. Wagner, attempting to find out the truth. Unaccompanied by Paula, George and Maria visited Wilhelm five times. They became increasingly concerned as they saw his physical condition deteriorating. Wilhelm's life seemed to be in jeopardy.

The doctor finally surrendered to George's relentless calling and pressured the physicians at Weissenhof for an answer. The Ziefles' suspicions proved correct. Before each visit from his relatives, Wilhelm was forced to swallow pills which induced his irrational behavior. There was nothing wrong with him—except that he had told the truth about the Führer. But the Nazis had no intentions of releasing Wilhelm; Maria would pray and weep much for her brother in the ensuing months.

As the days of autumn grew steadily colder, so did the attitudes of some of the pro-Nazi neighbors. Each afternoon as Maria took her stroll, she would encounter one or more acquaintance who zealously saluted and snapped, "Heil Hitler." She always smiled and nodded in return, but each time, the critical stares were more incisive. Herr Müller was the worst. He operated a small, noisy machine shop behind his house and thus prided himself on being the neighborhood industrialist. His salutes were drenched with mockery. And of course Herr Schmidt, the highest-ranking Nazi, always eyed her with suspicion.

Such encounters were proving to be too much for Maria, so she resorted to the cover of darkness for her nightly stroll. With George at her side, she would walk up and down the upper Ackermannstrasse for 15 or 20 minutes, getting as much exercise and fresh air as possible.

These were good times for the couple to discuss things privately. But even in the dark, deserted street, they spoke in whispers; they were now aliens, even in their own neighborhood.

As the weeks passed, the swelling of life inside Maria began to make itself plain. The camouflage of her bulky coat thus far had kept the matter secret from people, but she wondered how soon they would begin to notice.

The three children, still anticipating their "piggy," were unaware as well until one afternoon late in November. They were outside in the backyard, busying themselves with building a little barn for the future pet. Kurt came into the kitchen to get a drink. As he gulped the water, he observed his mother as she arched backwards, trying to stretch after stooping over her baking. Eyeing her expanding abdomen, he suddenly brightened up and blurted, "Mama, are you going to have a baby? Is that what you meant by a 'surprise'?"

She grinned sheepishly and nodded.

Kurt whirled, ran downstairs and out the door. "Reinhold! Ruth! We'd better get rid of this piggy barn. We're getting something much better—Mama's going to have a baby!"

The other two dropped their work and ran behind Kurt into the house and upstairs to the kitchen. They crowded around her, cheering and asking questions. Reinhold appeared slightly embarrassed that his younger brother had discovered the secret before he did. Kurt always seemed to be the bold, adventurous one.

Kurt, now 13, was enrolled in confirmation class at the Matthäuskirche. Many of the teenagers in the class were there against their will; deep-rooted religious traditions still influenced parents in the early Hitler years, even though most of the men no longer attended church. The children respected their parents' wishes and attended the classes, but, for most, their hearts were far from the catechism.

Pastor Brendle desperately attempted to teach his beliefs to the children, though most were not even faintly interested. They reacted with scorn and violence. The boys, especially, would jeer him, and encourage the girls to join in their misbehavior. Eventually, they were throwing hymnals at each other and the pastor and overturning tables and chairs in the classroom. Brendle tolerated them as best he could; complaints to parents or authorities would be useless.

In spite of Kurt's shallow regard for God's truth, he remained firm in his respect for authority. Concerned by the taunts of his classmates, he attempted to set a good example by helping the pastor pick up the books and set the furniture back in its place. Instead, this antagonized his peers.

"Don't you dare go home today!" growled one of the ringleaders to Kurt as the class was being dismissed. "We're going to beat you up."

Unperturbed, Kurt eyed him cooly and replied, "I'm not afraid of you. When are you going to start acting civilized?"

"You just wait!" the bully snapped as he whirled and stepped toward the door. Outside he gathered five of his cronies and waited at the gate in front of the church.

Also helping Pastor Brendle was a girl named Hilde. Kurt, somewhat bashfully, worked with her to finish cleaning the classroom. They bade their pastor good-bye and strolled out the door together. In front of them stood six of their classmates, with jaws and fists clenched.

Undaunted, Kurt marched straight toward the group with Hilde close behind. He stiff-armed the first boy's chest and grunted, "Get out of my way!" The two walked past the rest without another word. Kurt told his parents nothing of the incident.

Embarrassed by the episode, the six Lutheran boys gathered a large group of their Catholic friends to help teach Kurt a lesson. The next week, after he and Hilde had cleaned up the room and walked outside, they found themselves facing almost twenty boys, all trying to look as fierce as possible.

Without hesitating, Kurt and Hilde quickened their pace and stared straight ahead. The silent gangmembers raised their fists. The two passed through the pack, the boys standing as if frozen.

This time Kurt couldn't restrain himself when he arrived home. "Mama, when Hilde and I left confirmation class, there were nearly twenty bullies waiting to beat me up. We just walked right through them, and it was as—as if someone cast a spell on them. They didn't even move!"

Maria was glad for the chance to show that God was working in the life of the son for whom she was most concerned. "Don't you think that maybe God protected you? Maybe He sent angels to hold those boys so that they couldn't fight."

Embarrassed at the thought, Kurt turned and moved away. "Maybe, Mama. Maybe." Maria smiled. The Spirit was using even miracles to keep her son's weak faith from evaporating.

Her thoughts quickly jumped back to her encounter with Otto Steiner that morning in the bakery. For two weeks he had not stopped in for Dämmerstündle, so today she had made a point of asking him about it. He mysteriously changed the subject and never answered her question. She was concerned about the troubled expression on his face.

Lord, maybe your angels need to give Otto a miracle, too.

Soon after supper there was a loud knock at the door. Reinhold ran to answer. A few seconds later, his voice rang up the stairs, "Papa, it's Otto! He wants to talk to you!" George disappeared down the steps.

Otto kept his eyes toward the floor as George approached him. "Herr Ziefle, I've come to return your Bible—I won't be needing it anymore. I've been considering my future, and the only way that I can see opportunity for success is with the Nazis. They would not want me to have this."

He thrust the Bible into George's hands, whirled and bolted out the door. George did not even get his mouth open to answer.

"Maria!" George called as he trudged up the stairs. His voice heavy with disappointment, he held up the Bible as evidence. "We've lost Otto, Maria."

Maria hung her head and stood wringing her hands. "God be merciful to Otto. If it weren't for God's promise of protection, I would almost wish that the baby would not live through delivery. I don't want him to have to face the Nazis and lose his faith like Otto."

The troubling situation surrounding the family only aggravated Maria's physical problems. As her delivery date drew closer, she became increasingly weak. Housework was an exhausting trial, and the rounds to the stores for groceries became nearly impossible.

It was now early March, only a month to go. With George's coaxing and assistance, Maria painfully continued her nightly walks. Supporting her valiantly with his arms, George helped Maria as she dragged her feet toward Staufenbergstrasse, then back to the house.

One evening after they returned home and entered the living room to call the children for Dämmerstündle, they heard frantic knocking at the door. George quickly descended the stairs to answer. "Paula! What is the matter?" he exclaimed as he opened the door to his sister-in-law.

"Wilhelm can come home! He's being released!" she exclaimed as she stepped into the hallway, shivering with excitement. She paused for a moment then rushed toward the stairs.

"Maria! Did you hear?" she said breathlessly. "He can come home tomorrow!"

Maria was silent. Seated on the couch, she held her hands close to her face; her eyes were already glistening with tears. She motioned for Paula to sit beside her. Paula quickly came to her side, and they wept in each other's arms.

The next morning, George, Maria, and Paula nervously stepped out of their car and approached the main entrance of the mental hospital. As they stepped through the doorway and entered the lobby, an emaciated, bent figure approached them. The tall, strong Wilhelm they remembered was almost unrecognizable. Paula ran toward him and embraced and kissed him; they had not touched for six months.

Wilhelm finally stepped away from his wife and approached his sister and brother-in-law. Weakly, he placed his arms around them. "Thank you." His voice was thin and raspy. "Thank you for helping us, for getting my release."

Maria sniffed quietly and squeezed him harder. "We worked, but God made the way. It's a miracle you are even alive."

"You're right, Sister. You're right."

Slowly the four made their way out of the building to the car. Hardly able to comprehend his new freedom, Wilhelm sat and stared at the countryside as they drove toward

Sontheim. The others were too happy to speak. In a short while the four had gathered around the dining room table at the Ziefles' house.

Wilhelm, unsteady from his ordeal, held his coffee cup with both hands. "When the Gestapo arrested me at the factory," he began, "the officers grabbed me and threw me down on the floor. They held me down while one of them kicked me several times. I screamed in pain, and one of them shouted to the workers who watched, 'See, he is insane!'

"As soon as I was brought to Weissenhof, they tied me in a strait-jacket and pushed me into the cell. I was already in great pain and could hardly move. One of the officers began describing what a terrible crime I had committed against the Fatherland and promised that I would be severely punished. I told him, 'You can't make me feel guilty for telling the truth. I demand that you let me go.'

"The men became furious. One of them shouted, 'You Schweinehund! We'll teach you who is in authority!' The officers pulled me to my feet and began to beat me with their fists until I was bruised all over. They threw me against the wall and I collapsed. Then they just walked out and locked the cell door.

"I hardly slept that night because of the pain. The next morning two aides came in and dragged me to a surgical room. They strapped me onto a table and, without giving me any anesthesia, they—" Wilhelm stared into his coffee. His voice barely audible, he murmured, "They castrated me. They didn't want my 'bad genes' to be passed on." He sat silent for a few moments as the horror dawned on his three listeners.

"It was several days before the pain was gone. When I finally felt strong again, I told some aides, 'Someday, you will pay for what you have done to me.' They became very angry and beat me. I still don't remember many details after that.

"I finally became so sick and weak that I was sure I

would die. I had not been a very good Christian before, but I cried out to God like never before, and asked Him to help me and to free me from the torture. I spent much time talking to God after that. It was the only way I kept my sanity.''

George interrupted. ''Do you have any idea why they finally released you?''

''I'm not sure what prompted them to do it, but two days ago a pair of aides came to my cell and escorted me to the director's office. The director ordered me to sit down; then for a long time he sat writing at his desk, totally ignoring me.

''Finally, he glared at me and shouted, 'Glaser, insulting our beloved Führer is a detestable crime! You deserve to be exterminated.' I was certain that my life was over then. I just stared at the floor.

''The director became even angrier and screamed, 'Are you sorry for what you did?'

''I was speechless. I didn't understand why he would ask me that. Suddenly I sensed a voice telling me not to offend this man. So I told him I was sorry.

''He said, 'If you promise not to criticize the great Führer any more, you will be a free man in two days.' I gladly promised him that—at least I won't criticize him publicly!''

''I believe it was a miracle,'' declared Maria. ''Let's thank God for it right now.''

All four were overflowing with praise as they voiced their gratitude to the Deliverer. Maria listened with deep joy to Wilhelm and Paula. The ordeal had brought them both to a total surrender of their lives to God.

Maria's spirit was strengthened through her brother's homecoming, but her body continued to weaken. Later that week, she had so little stamina that the doctor admitted her to the hospital for rest and intravenous feeding. Dr. Picard, as all Jewish physicians in Germany, had now been barred from his practice. Maria was under the care of Dr. Schramm, who lived near the Ziefle home. The baby was not due for three weeks.

Maria had lost much weight, and her family and friends became alarmed at her condition. But despite the strain on her body, her spirit was resolute. Ernst Veigel, a Christian friend, noted, "Frau Ziefle, there is no question in my mind you will survive. Through your eyes I see much faith and fight in you. You are a strong woman."

The wait was painful for mind and body. Maria felt helpless as she lay in the bed, unable to be home guiding her children and aiding her husband. Even George began to look a bit tired. *He needs some of my gruel that he likes so well,* she told herself.

But the Almighty stood by, His presence no surprise to a woman who spoke intimately with Him daily.

Maria regained enough strength so that she was allowed to return home to wait for her child's birth. On April 2, 1939, Palm Sunday, Maria felt the first contractions beginning. George soon called for the midwife. Five minutes before midnight the Ziefle children had a new brother, somewhat skinny but healthy. They all agreed on the name Helmut and shared great ambitions to spoil him in every way possible. Maria's time and thoughts were now concentrated on caring for her new child. And George proudly told everyone of his little Helmut.

Life and innocence were cause for celebration in the Ziefle house. The hate and suspicion that surrounded them were temporarily forgotten.

III

September 1939

We ARE barbarians! We want to be KNOWN as
barbarians!

—Adolf Hitler

The Volksempfänger[6] crackled to life as the thumping
beat of march music faded. "Achtung! Achtung! The
Wehrmacht[7] has repulsed Polish attacks on Germany's
border. The armies of the Third Reich have now invaded
Poland. We will not tolerate violations of our territory! Stay
tuned for further developments. Heil Hitler!"

Pale and shaken, George Ziefle sat silently before the radio. Not wanting to hear more, he finally leaned forward
and switched it off. Shaking his head from side to side, he
murmured, "Our Germany is headed for her doom. I can
feel it."

"Please, Papa!" Maria pleaded in a hoarse whisper.
"The children." Maria raised her voice. "Reinhold, Kurt—
tell me some more about your work in the harvest this summer." Attempting to change the subject was useless; the
boys were more interested in the war. Maria finally herded
them outside to play.

But outside, the neighborhood was buzzing excitedly
over the prospect of a new war. Powerless to protect her

---

6. "People's Radio."
7. The German armed forces.

children from the winds of war, Maria watched anxiously as innocent minds were entranced with the romance of conflict without comprehending the bloodshed and destruction.

It was September 1, 1939. In Sontheim and throughout Germany, the Third Reich had come of age.

Two days later France and England declared war against Germany. The call to arms ensnared able-bodied men wherever the swastika cast its shadow. Maria Ziefle now faced the additional fear of a fatherless family.

But the uncertainty did not last long; within a few days, George received orders to join the Wehrmacht.

Maria could no longer maintain the rigid exterior that had successfully protected her tender spirit. As she sat alone in the house nursing little Helmut, she wept silently—for her husband and her children and especially for this little one. And she prayed:

I do not understand why all this is happening to us, but because you are God, I trust you. Somehow, Lord, make a way for George not to have to fight, actually not to kill people! Yesterday, when he told the Wehrmacht officers that it was against his conscience to bear arms, I thanked you for such a bold husband. But I am really afraid, Lord, that maybe they will imprison him now. Whatever happens, take care of us, please.

Nervously the family waited during the next days for Wehrmacht's answer. On the last Friday of September the final answer came. As Maria pulled the letters out of the mailbox and shuffled through them, she suddenly stopped, feeling weak. It was a letter from the draft board—she was going to lose her husband.

But Maria was mistaken. After her trembling fingers got the envelope open, inside were orders for George to report to the Red Cross station on Wilhelmstrasse in Heilbronn— little more than a mile from home. It seemed like an impossible dream! She impatiently waited for him to arrive home that evening.

George returned from work that day looking worn, his face reflecting frustration and worry. Maria called to him as she heard him slowly climbing the stairs. "Papa! We have good news! The draft board sent orders for you to report to the Red Cross."

George's pace miraculously quickened and he hurried into the kitchen where his wife stood. With a cautious smile he asked, "Are you serious, Mama?"

"There's the letter on the table; read it for yourself."

He snatched up the letter and read it quickly, trembling. "It's true! I won't have to fight!" He put his arms around his wife exuberantly. "Our prayers are answered! He is still taking care of us!"

Maria nodded happily, her joy and relief evident in her smile.

Poland was now trampled by the German blitzkrieg[8], and most of the people of Sontheim, as across Germany, were ecstatic with their apparent invincibility. But George and Maria were not deceived. After all, why would more and more men have to be pressed into the Red Cross emergency service if Germany's armed forces were having overwhelming success? It made no sense to men who viewed the world with a sense of reason.

George's Red Cross duty began with several weeks of training, and allowed no visits at home. Maria was granted only one visit each week.

Morale in the Ziefle home waned in spite of their happiness at George's duty. Maria was forced not only to shoulder all the responsibilities of the household, but she constantly had to bolster the children's spirits as they begged, "When will Papa come home?"

George appeared at home unexpectedly on a Sunday in mid-November. Maria was preparing lunch after church when she heard his footsteps coming up the stairs. She ran

8. Lightning war.

to greet him. "George! Why are you home? And you're so thin!"

"The food—it's been very hard on my stomach. I've been sick for several days, so Dr. Wagner gave me permission to eat at home from now on. And training is almost over, so soon I'll be off-duty every other day. I think your cooking will get me back to full strength, Mama."

"I'm so glad, George! What would you like for lunch?"

"Just some gruel. That's all I can take right now."

The three older children came in from playing. "Papa!" they cried as they ran to embrace him. Surrounding him with their arms and happy chatter, they began probing about his activities, as well as reporting to him all their recent accomplishments.

When the encounter with the three oldest children had subsided, he stole into his bedroom to see his youngest son. Five weeks had passed since he had been with any of the children. The twilight of the room and the innocence of the sleeping baby soothed him. *How can there be such peace here in the midst of war and hate,* he thought to himself. *God, you have answered my prayers. Thank you for taking good care of my family.*

When he returned to the living room upstairs, George noticed Ruth slouched on the deacon's bench, dejectedly paging through one of her favorite books. Puzzled, he asked, "What's wrong, Ruth? You look as if your best friend just left you."

"When I was playing in the street this morning, Herr Koch stopped and yelled at me for not saying 'Heil Hitler' and saluting right. He said I'd go to prison if I continued to disobey him. He always stops and threatens me."

"Well, how do you salute him?" George inquired.

"I raise my hand as if I'm going to catch a fly on my face, then I drop it right away. Ever since I had to join Jung Mädchen[9] this year, I've had to salute, even though I don't

---

9. Young Maidens—the girls' division of Hitler Youth.

want to." Ruth's voice quivered as she began to whimper. "I'm so scared of Herr Koch that when I see him coming down the street I try to hide, but I never get away in time."

George put his arm around his daughter and led her into the dining room where his gruel was waiting. After bowing to pray for his meal, he began to eat, counseling Ruth between mouthfuls, "Ruth, I don't want you to worry about going to prison. Your mother and I are here to protect you from that. Besides, they're more interested in arresting adults than nice young girls."

"But he's so mean to me. He grabs my arm so hard that it hurts, and he curses at me." She looked at her father through her tears.

"Listen, I'm proud of you. Do you know that? You are standing up for what's right, even when everyone else is giving in to the Nazi lies. I'm certain even God is proud of you!

"Herr Koch is a man we should feel sorry for and pray for. He gets drunk very often, and I'm sure he's very unhappy. Even though he is a Nazi official, I've heard that he can hardly read—you can do better than that. I think he doesn't really care as much about the Nazis as about himself. If the communists were in control, he would probably become a communist just as easily as he has become a Nazi."

George gathered the family at the table for a time of prayer. They prayed for George's health, for their own unity, for Pastor Brendle—and for Herr Koch, Ruth's tormentor.

It was time for George to return to the Red Cross station. At least from now on he could be home every other day, and for all meals. George enjoyed his duties at the Red Cross. Dr. Wagner and Dr. Baumann, his superiors, were impressed with his sense of responsibility and his honesty, so they treated him well. George had been assigned to drive one of the ambulances—a van capable of carrying up to six injured people. He gave his vehicle meticulous care, keeping it ready for use at all times.

Winter that year was quiet for the Ziefles. George regained his health after he began eating Maria's carefully planned meals again. The pressures of the Nazi presence had not subsided, but the family was learning to live under the cloud of criticism and intimidation. Reinhold still refused to participate in Hitler Youth meetings, and he and Ruth continued to attend Sunday services with their parents as long as the church remained open. Kurt insisted on being faithful to his Jungvolk activities.

The headiness of the citizens after Poland's demolition had subsided, and the war now seemed to be a matter of necessary inconvenience. After all, the armies of the Third Reich would soon smother all of Europe and then peace would be permanent. But life was not normal, by far. Many of the eligible men had been conscripted into service, leaving their families without fathers and husbands. The women of Sontheim did their best to cope without their husbands, but the struggle was very evident in their faces.

Life was hardest for those who refused to compromise their beliefs and cooperate with National Socialism. The psychological and physical pressures were strong, and many times the faith of even the strong collapsed.

Though the Third Reich was continually touted as invincible, the Nazis began to show an increased concern for the safety of the citizens in the event of an air attack. Even at the beginning of the war, people were ordered to keep their houses blacked out after dark. Now, however, the government had initiated an extensive air-raid-shelter program.

By early 1940, the people of Sontheim were fully involved in developing shelters. To cooperate with the program, the Ziefles began by removing all flammable materials from their attic, to prevent fueling a fire should a bomb ever strike their home. As soon as the rooms were cleared of newspapers, books and other items, workers from the city hall sprayed the interiors of the attic and cellar with a fire-resistant solution. The neighborhood air warden inspected the results and gave official approval, after which he provided a fire extinguisher and gas masks to be stored in the cellar.

The Ziefles' cellar was well suited for an air-raid shelter. Though it lacked large emergency exits, its yard-thick stone walls and heavily-timbered ceiling gave it a vault-like quality. George and his sons set about to equip the refuge properly. First they obtained concrete slabs which they positioned over the cellar windows. Then they constructed a half-dozen bunk beds which they "upholstered" with straw mattresses and pillows.

"I sure hope we won't have to use this place," Kurt declared. "The smell would drive me insane." The briny sauerkraut, the vegetables and meat (we had no refrigerator), and Krauters' two wine barrels gave the cellar an atmosphere that sent even the stout-hearted reeling.

"If bombs are falling all around," Reinhold replied, "you won't even think about the smell."

Kurt stiffened and answered resolutely, "The enemy planes will never be allowed to enter Germany. Our armies are too powerful!"

"I hope you're right," his father said quietly.

However, English scout planes soon began to fly over the Heilbronn area. The city held a large railroad center and considerable manufacturing; it was a likely target for an enemy bent on crippling a nation. Anti-aircraft guns had been used several times to repel the planes, but since the aircraft kept at high altitude, such weapons had little effect.

When the war had broken out, the Heilbronn area was armed with five anti-aircraft batteries for a total of 28 guns—far from adequate for Heilbronn and its suburbs. Heilbronn alone was home to over 70,000 people. The 34th infantry regiment—the Heilbronn garrison—had been withdrawn in August of 1939 to prepare for an offensive on the Western Front. The local citizens were becoming increasingly concerned with the possibility of their community being a military target without protection.

In addition to converting private cellars for shelters, the Nazis began to construct large public facilities for those who had no cellars or for those caught too far from their houses. Large commercial wine cellars were commandeered for the purpose. One shelter near the Matthäuskirche could hold 2,000 people.

By July 1940, the air battles over England were in full fury. As the Ziefles read their newspapers and listened to radio broadcasts, they were given nothing but predictions of a quick victory.

One warm evening as George turned off the radio, he commented to Maria, "This seems so strange to me—if the war is going to be won so soon, why are the Nazis building all these air-raid shelters? They're working so furiously to have enough capacity; and, in their hurry, they're building shelters that I don't think are strong enough to withstand heavy bombing. That new one we pass on the way to church has both entrances so close together that one bomb could trap all the occupants. It looks to me as if we're facing the prospect of a long war."

"I expect you're right," Maria replied, sounding worried. "If that happens, what about our boys? It won't be long before they will be eligible for the draft. If they are taken into the service, what will happen to them—especially Kurt? We can help anchor their souls when they are here, but what can we do when they are in an army camp far away?"

Just then there was a knock at the door. George hurried to answer. As he opened the door he was addressed with a stiff, "Heil Hitler!"

"Oh, it is you, Herr Müller," George answered flatly.

"Herr Ziefle, I must speak with you and your wife immediately." His voice was cold.

"Why—certainly. Come upstairs." George led him to the living room. He wondered as to the nature of the visit. Müller was now the precinct captain for the Nazi Party.

Perhaps he was on his fund-raising rounds.

"Heil Hitler, Frau Ziefle," he greeted as he approached Maria, who was seated on the couch. "We are disturbed that the two of you do not involve yourselves in our Nazi cause. We know that you do not contribute money, but we are even more concerned that you do not attend any of our meetings. I realize, Herr Ziefle, that your duties with the Red Cross prevent you from attendance. However, your wife has proven her disrespect for the Party by not attending at all, so the Party demands an explanation. You have two weeks to present your case to the committee. Use your time well. I will return in a few days."

Müller whirled and disappeared through the door. George and Maria looked at each other in silent bewilderment as they listened to the man's boots clomp heavily down the stairs.

Maria grasped her husband's hand and pulled him down next to her. Biting her lip she slowly shook her head. "Papa, I could go to prison for this—or be publicly humiliated."

"Not as long as I'm alive," George assured steadily. He took both her hands in his. They sat silently, each mentally presenting their dilemma to God.

"I think the Lord has given me an idea," George exclaimed, giving his wife's hands a squeeze. "You've been having problems with phlebitis for all these years, and since Helmut's birth, it's been worse. Maybe if Dr. Wagner examined you, he could verify that you are physically unable to attend the meetings. Then the Nazis would leave you alone!"

George's good relationship with his superiors was rewarded. Three days later Dr. Wagner examined Maria and recommended to the Party officials that she be excused from meetings for health reasons. His advice was accepted and Maria was no longer troubled regarding the meetings.

German optimism waxed strong as Nazi forces swept across Denmark and Norway on the north and France on the west. Encouraged by Hitler's victories, Mussolini also declared war against the Allies. As the German victories mounted, Maria noticed that neighbors who had been lukewarm or indifferent toward Hitler began to increase in apparent loyalty and fervor for the Führer.

The Nazis were no longer persecuting only Jews and staunch Christians, but anyone who refused to accept the "Deutschglaube"[10] as the only and ultimate religion. Deutschglaube had its roots in 2,000-year-old Germanic folklore which glorified national heroism, purity of race, and German destiny to rule the world. Anyone who deviated from these Nazi ideals was either re-educated, harassed, imprisoned or sometimes even exiled or murdered.

The Nazis exhibited little respect for an individual's ability, experience, or character as they appointed people to positions of leadership in government and business. Party loyalty was all that mattered. Older Storm Troopers, such as the alcoholic Herr Koch, were the prime candidates for leadership in those days.

The bank president in Sontheim had been replaced by a Nazi who would not, under normal conditions, even qualify as a clerk. Factory owners who refused to join the party also were being replaced. It was only a matter of time before Dr. Ackermann, owner of the large local textile mill, would be evicted from his own office.

Maria considered these matters as she sat in front of her house and watched the children play with Helmut. What could a parent do to instill in one's children values of decency, respect, faithfulness and diligence, when all around the only thing that seemed to guarantee success was the rejection of such qualities? She presented her frustrations to her God. *I have no doubt, Lord, that your grace is sufficient. But I doubt myself; is my faith sufficient to endure these times?*

In the midst of social turmoil and the tension of war,

---

10. Faith in the Germanic way of life.

Maria had to laugh as she watched Kurt whirl Helmut about their small yard in the battered stroller. There was still happiness in their midst; love and innocence still survived under Maria and George's strong determination. But how long would it last? The swastika never retreated; rather, it made itself increasingly more evidente as it laid siege against the Ziefle household.

By God's mercy I have not lost my husband to the war, but what about Reinhold and Kurt? What about the demands for conformity upon Ruth? And will Helmut enter manhood knowing only war cries and persecution? Life would never be as it was, but how Maria longed to return to the times of peace.

She reflected back to the time that seemed like years ago, to the moments right after the appalling announcement that Germany had invaded Poland. As Maria had attempted to divert the children's attention from the gruesome subject, Reinhold, his young face filled with bewilderment, had asked, "Papa, what is war?"

IV
Autumn 1941

The Jews are a parasite race which lives on the cultures of healthy nations like mildew. Against this only one remedy helps: make a cut and push it off. Merciless coldness!

—Joseph Goebbels,
Nazi minister of propaganda

"Mama!" Kurt called as he rushed into the kitchen, still gripping his school bag. "The Brown Shirts are beating up Dr. Picard in his house!"

Maria abruptly stopped her work. "Who told you this?"

"I just walked past his house, and I could hear yelling and screaming, and a noise like someone was being hit! I know it was the Brown Shirts, because I saw the emblems on their bicycles."

"Oh, Kurt, is there something we can do?" asked Maria, urgency in her voice. Somberly answering her question, she looked into Kurt's eyes, "All we can do right now is to wait for your father to come home. And he won't be back until seven tonight."

Maria went back to her cooking, praying for the elderly physician as she stirred. A man in his mid-seventies could easily die from such abuse. But in her heart she also rejoiced over Kurt's intense concern for the Jewish doctor; it was a good sign that he still had not succumbed to the Nazis' anti-Semitism.

She remembered her conversation with Kurt a few weeks earlier as they were walking home from the bakery on Mauerstrasse. "Mama, there's something that bothers me about the Nazis."

"Oh?" She tried to act disinterested.

"You know how I like to go to the city hall each week and read the newest *Stürmer*—especially the section about the sports activities of the Hitler Youth. And I really enjoy Jungvolk meetings, but—but there is so much hate toward the Jews. The Nazis accuse the Jews of being enemies of Germany, but all the Jews we know are good people—like Dr. Picard. He is always so nice to me."

Thank you, Lord, that the fire of love is still burning in Kurt's heart. I'm amazed he has not yet become a hateful Nazi.

When George arrived home, he immediately read the worry on Maria's face. "What is the matter, Mama?"

"It's Dr. Picard. Kurt walked by his house today and thought he heard the Brown Shirts beating him up."

"Those scoundrels! They go around like a pack of dogs and destroy helpless, innocent people!" George turned and stormed out the living room door. "I'm going to do something about this!"

"Don't do anything foolish," Maria warned helplessly.

George glanced around him to make sure no one was looking, then approached the door of Dr. Picard's large villa. He tapped the door quietly.

"Who is it?" a voice called weakly.

"George Ziefle. Do you need any help, Doctor?"

Picard slowly opened the door. Almost unrecognizable, his face was purple with huge welts, and mottled with dried blood. His eyes were nearly swollen shut.

"Herr Ziefle, thank God you are here! I must leave Germany immediately before the Brown Shirts come again." His voice was low and hoarse. "Will you buy some of my furniture so that I can purchase a ticket for America?"

George did not hesitate. Stepping inside, he answered, "Certainly. When should I come and get it?"

"Come after ten o'clock, when fewer people are on the street. If those thugs catch us, they're apt to throw us both in prison."

"Will you come and have supper with us, Doctor?"

"I wish I could, but I must say good-bye to some other friends before you return tonight. I will never forget this kindness, Herr Ziefle. But you must leave now. I don't want you in trouble for my sake."

Dr. Picard escaped Germany with his life; but the Ziefles were saddened that Germany had lost a faithful citizen. Other "enemies" of the party were not so fortunate. Arrests of such people were on the increase. Being caught criticizing the Nazi Party or listening to foreign radio broadcasts meant almost certain imprisonment and sometimes death. Increasingly, violence was no longer limited to the night hours.

The war continued to escalate. Germany had already been fighting with Russia for several months, and there was rumor of future conflict with the United States. The radio announcers continually glorified German victories in Denmark, Belgium, and France. In June, pictures of German soldiers in Paris appeared in the newspaper, and in July the air attack on England commenced.

And in Sontheim itself the war also was edging closer. Several times during the summer, air-raid sirens had sounded two short blasts—enemy planes had been sighted flying toward unknown targets in southern Germany.

It was on a late Sunday night in mid-October when Maria, alone in bed, was again awakened by two short warning blasts. She stumbled across the dark room, found her robe and slipped it on. Hurrying up the stairs to the attic, she called, "Reinhold! Kurt! To the cellar!"

Kurt sleepily answered, "Mama, we're not afraid. Nothing has happened to Sontheim yet. Please let us stay in bed."

Reluctantly, Maria gave in. "Just make sure that if you hear the full alarm—or planes—you'll come to the cellar immediately."

"Yes, Mama."

She quickly went downstairs, woke Ruth and picked up two-and-a-half-year-old Helmut from his bed. By candle-light the three nervously descended to the cellar and tried to make themselves comfortable on the straw mattresses. Ruth and Helmut quickly fell asleep, but their mother lay tense in the dark, pungent dampness. Their neighbors, the Krauters, had not come down either; Maria surmised that they also were ignoring the sirens.

An hour passed in silence. Then two hours. It was now after midnight. Suddenly the sirens came to life. Would it be the long all-clear, or the minute-long blasts of the full alarm? Maria, poised to run for her sons, listened as the first wailing blast began to die and a second began. She leaped from the bunk and shook Ruth. "Watch Helmut. I'm going to get the boys!"

As she reached the cellar door a deafening explosion made the house shudder. Maria, her heart pounding, rushed up the stairway screaming, "Reinhold! Kurt!"

"We're coming! We're coming!" Sleep having gone as quickly as the explosion, the frantic teenagers scurried down, their bare feet slapping on the wooden steps. They rushed breathlessly through the door and Maria closed the latch behind them. Shivering in their pajamas, the boys listened to a strange new sound—the eerie whistling of a descending bomb, then another thudding explosion.

"Boys," Maria spoke sternly, "the next time you hear a warning siren, you will immediately come to the cellar. Is that clear?"

Their mother's instructions had never been so clear. They replied sheepishly, "We will, Mama. We will."

"Children, we must pray for your father. He may be busy tonight, and work could be very dangerous." They all knelt down next to the bunks.

Even Helmut lisped his simple request, "God, take care of Papa."

The explosions stopped after only a few minutes, as suddenly as they had begun. The silence seemed almost as threatening as the explosions. Finally the all-clear sirens began their wail—a long, sustained blast. Maria led her little family back to their rooms.

In a few minutes Maria lay under her covers, vainly trying to ease the tension in her body. She chuckled nervously as she recalled the frequently broadcast statement by Hermann Göring, supreme commander of the Luftwaffe, "My name is nothing if even one enemy plane crosses the German border."

The next morning, after George safely returned for breakfast, the family went to survey the damage. The first hit had been only a half-mile from their house; an incendiary bomb had devastated a private home. Reinhold, awed by the smoldering wreckage, murmured, "If that had hit our house, Kurt, you and I would both be dead. I'll never ignore another siren."

The Heilbronn area was attacked again after seven weeks, but damage was relatively light. The citizens comforted themselves with the possibility that the enemy was losing its potency and soon their worries would be over. But four days later, Germany declared war on the United States—a strange, faraway enemy, with a huge country and almost unlimited resources. The rhetoric of optimism was ringing very hollow indeed.

But it was not the bombs and the realities of war that taxed one's endurance. It was the strain of coping in the midst of an oppressive society. Good friends now eyed each other with suspicion. Kindness was an act of weakness. Loyalty to conscience was treason. Most of the Ziefles had already entrenched themselves against this onslaught of evil, of moral decay. And they had sadly, with great concern, watched Kurt and his enthusiasm for the new order. But now it was beginning to wear thin for him, too. The warmth of love in his home had kept something alive inside him. And it wasn't just the matter of the Jews. He was only 14, and already pressures that could crack a man were closing in on him.

Recognizing his physical prowess and his sharp mind, the Hitler Youth directors had appointed Kurt to a leadership position in his group. In athletic competition, Kurt was always one of the winners, and when they played war games, his group would rally under his natural leadership abilities and defeat their competitors.

The weekly meetings were two- and three-hour yelling sessions. They were kept at a high emotional pitch with songs and loud exhortations on excellence, while the boys stood rigidly at attention or goose-stepped like Storm Troopers for an hour at a time. The pressure to succeed drained Kurt.

Kurt was no longer able to attend school, for he had taken a man's job. So much manpower had been diverted to the war that businesses began drawing personnel from those below draft age. Kurt was hired as a clerk at the Kreissparkasse Bank in Heilbronn. The job was exciting at first, but the work load and responsibilities began to increase.

In addition to his work there, his troubles were compounded by some of the young women employees. Several of them had begun making romantic advances toward him; and at his young age, Kurt was confused and frustrated further.

Inside, he was in turmoil. The Nazis had fostered too much pride in his soul for him to admit his troubles to his parents. He had nowhere to turn. He finally reached the breaking point on New Year's Day, 1942, just a few days before his fifteenth birthday. Kurt had worked all day and into the night figuring interest rates. He came home, and after a few hours of troubled sleep, he quietly left the house with a small bag of clothes under his arm. With a sense of desperation, he rode the streetcar to the train station. Pretending to be on bank business, he purchased a ticket to Stuttgart. From there he made connections to Friedrichstadt, Innsbruck, and finally to Feldkirch, a little village on the Swiss border. There a tall barbed-wire fence stood between him and freedom.

Unsure as to how to cross the border and without money to rent a room, he slept for two nights in restaurants while trying to formulate a plan. Unfortunately, he had been reported to the border patrol as a suspicious person, and on the third day he was stopped by the police. The policemen checked his identification and made a call to Sontheim. Kurt was arrested as a deserter and escorted back to his hometown.

George and Maria, in great distress over their son's disappearance, had called the bank and many of his friends, but had received no clues as to his whereabouts. When the authorities called and told him to take his son home, George, with great relief, hurried to the police station. But for many weeks, Kurt remained silent about his attempted escape; he was still too proud to admit weakness.

To Kurt's amazement, as well as the family's, he was not disciplined by the Hitler Youth leaders. Herr Betz, the director, lied about the incident and told everyone that Kurt had attempted to join the army in Italy. He even arranged for Kurt to attend a ski course which was reserved exclusively for soldiers. Upon returning, Kurt was restored to second-in-command, directly under Betz. The Nazis were desperate for good leadership. Though the youngest in the group, Kurt's physical strength and reputation gained him much respect from his fellow Hitler Youth.

With Kurt in the forefront, Reinhold's absence from the meetings was increasingly obvious. At school and on the street, his friends and Hitler Youth leaders continually hounded him about the matter. In April he finally gave in.

At his first meeting, the boys stood at attention during the roll call. Suddenly Betz screamed, "Reinhold Ziefle! Why has it taken you so long to show up for the Hitler

Youth meetings? You were ordered to do so a year ago!''

Reinhold, intimidated by the shouting and by the forty-five Hitler Youth staring at him, remained silent. Furiously Betz stormed toward him, his fist raised to strike Reinhold's face. The gymnasium was silent. The man stood before Reinhold, seething, his fist still poised. The boys eagerly waited to see what their leader would do.

Reinhold lifted his arm to protect himself. Betz realized he was no match for the muscular boy, and that Kurt, who was even stronger, would no doubt leap to his brother's defense. Humiliated, the leader stepped back and resumed the roll call.

Eager for revenge, Betz reported Reinhold's delinquency to higher authorities, and Reinhold was quickly demoted to the Compulsory Hitler Youth. Most of the boys there were half-Jews and did their training under the scrutiny of the German police. Here Reinhold was treated as a second-class citizen; he became increasingly embittered against the Nazis.

In that same month of 1942, Reinhold, now almost 17, completed his middle school studies and became a commercial apprentice in a small dry-goods store in Heilbronn. Wilhelm Schmidt, the proprietor, made little effort to teach him how to manage the store, so Reinhold spent most days performing only odd tasks.

But Reinhold was fascinated with truth. He was not afraid to defy the Nazis, and began making every effort to discover what was really occurring in the world. The Nazis censored all information that came in the newspapers and on the radio; so, to satisfy his hunger, Reinhold began secretly to modify the family's Volksempfänger to receive shortwave broadcasts from England. Listening to such broadcasts was, of course, illegal, so he also set about building earphones from materials he could salvage.

He finally completed his project at the end of April. He would test the unit in his attic bedroom after midnight, to insure that Kurt would not find out. He eagerly waited in his bed one night until he heard the 12:30 chimes of the clock in the living room below. He silently rose to his feet and picked up the radio which was hidden in a box. Seated in the darkness as far from Kurt as possible, Reinhold plugged the unit into the wall socket and switched it on, pulling the headphones over his ears.

Static carried across the room, and then the faraway sound of a voice. Kurt began to stir, and finally sat up, vainly blinking in an attempt to see through the blackness. "What are you doing? Why are you listening to the radio in the middle of the night?" he muttered.

Reinhold, overjoyed with his success, whispered incautiously, "Quiet, I'm getting a broadcast from England!"

"Are you crazy?" Kurt jumped out of bed. "Don't you know you could end up in jail for this?"

"I don't care. I'm tired of hearing lies about victory. I'm going to find the truth, even if the Nazis kill me! I want freedom like they have in the West."

"I could never do what you're doing," Kurt said thoughtfully. "But I promised I won't betray you—you're my brother. Please be careful, though! The Nazis would be more than happy to shoot you—if you're caught."

Reinhold listened a while longer, then pulled the headphones from his head and switched off the radio. "Poor signal tonight. Maybe it won't fade out so much tomorrow." He felt his way back to the bed and began to crawl in. "Kurt, I appreciate your keeping this a secret. You're a great brother."

Kurt, already falling asleep, grunted acknowledgment. Reinhold lay tingling with the thrill of success. Now he would know the truth. The clock below chimed once.

The warm winds of spring were beginning to soften the countryside with new life now. Gardens and fields were green again, and the hedges and colorful flowers fascinated Helmut, who had just turned three. He was now old enough to appreciate the beauty around him but, fortunately, unable to comprehend the miseries of war and the brutalities of the Nazis.

But 1942 was the quietest year of the war for the Ziefles, despite its traumatic beginning when Kurt tried to flee the country. Though life was becoming harsher, both physically and socially, the pressures seemed to escalate more slowly. Air raids were almost nonexistent, except for one in early May, when seven people in the area were killed.

For the children, one of the hardest situations to cope with at this time was the mounting scarcity of nonessential food items. Most such items were either diverted to the fighting fronts or else stockpiled by the Nazi leaders for their own use. Though staples also were in short supply, the children had the most difficulty adjusting to the lack of chocolate and other candies that formerly filled rows of glass jars in the stores with color and aroma.

For the Ziefle children, there was one small box of hard candies which Maria guarded for special use on birthdays, Christmas, and Easter. Two days after Christmas, Helmut approached her with a forlorn expression, "Mama, can't we have some more candy on New Year's Day?"

It was hard to refuse such a plaintive request. "I'm sorry, Helmut, but you'll have to wait about three more months until your birthday. Then you can choose two more candies from the box."

"Is that a long time, Mama?"

She smiled at his innocence. "It is for a three-year-old boy. But you'll just have to be patient." Even the children's candy was not immune from the shadow of Hitler's regime.

Before long the inconveniences broadened to include far more essential commodities. As the war effort heightened, the government confiscated the Ziefles' automobile. Private citizens were no longer allowed to own cars. The Ziefles' BMW was turned over to a doctor.

As Reinhold continued to listen surreptitiously to the news from England, he became firmly convinced that Germany faced certain defeat against the superior resources of the Allies. Nearly eighteen now, he was very concerned about being drafted into the German armed forces. Early in January, he admitted his fears to Kurt. "What will happen to me if I'm drafted? You're second-in-command in the Hitler Youth, but what about me? I don't even know how to handle a gun, let alone hit a target. Will you help me to be ready when they draft me?"

Kurt was glad to assist his brother and began to teach him basic military skills. Neither knew how timely this decision was. Though Reinhold was still only seventeen, two weeks later an envelope from the draft board appeared in the mail, addressed to him. He opened it slowly, finally pulling out the letter. The entire family was silently standing around him as he quickly scanned the message.

Dejected, he looked up. "I'm to report to the Reichsarbeitsdienst[11] on Tuesday, the twenty-first." He looked at his family, groping for words to express his feelings, "Now—now I won't be able to complete my apprenticeship."

No one was more disappointed over Reinhold's induction than his mother. Even at the initial announcement, her eyes became moist. She said as little as possible, even to George; but on the nights when he was on duty, she would lie on her bed and silently weep at the thought of losing her firstborn—putting his life in the custody of a government with no respect for life or its Creator.

Dämmerstündle on the evening of January 20 was a somber event. The possibility that this could be their final time together as a family was obvious to all of them. They knelt in a circle about Reinhold and committed him to God's keeping. Even Kurt could not restrain tears that night. And three-year-old Helmut, sensing in his spirit what his mind did not comprehend, gave Reinhold an extra-long hug.

The next morning, Maria, Kurt, Ruth, and Helmut so-

---

11. Hitler's labor service.

berly walked with Reinhold toward the Kolpingstrasse streetcar stop. George had already said his good-bye, unable to get time off from his job.

Inwardly, Maria cried for strength, but she did her best to make the farewell as pleasant as possible. She held Reinhold's arm tightly. "Son, remain strong in your faith. You know that God is everywhere and He will be with you." She hesitated as she strained to stifle her emotions. "Even though I can't be with you, my prayers and all that I've taught you—"

"Mama, please don't worry about me. I can face today because God gives me strength—and I'll always depend on Him. He will take good care of me—right, Mama?"

Maria forced a tearful smile and squeezed his arm. "I'm proud of you; and God will keep you. I'm sure He will." She wasn't nearly as certain in her heart. She had no doubts about God's role; but the pressures on Reinhold would be so great. . . .

The streetcar came clanking down the street and the sad party hurried toward the stop. They all wrapped their arms about him together. As the rest stepped back, Maria held him close and kissed him. The tears on their cheeks mixed together. Reluctantly she dropped her arms and Reinhold stepped briskly toward the car, clutching his bag.

The four on the street silently watched as Reinhold paid his fare and hurried to a seat next to a curbside window. With loud creaks and groans, the streetcar began to roll away. Reinhold lifted his hand and smiled sadly at his family. His loved ones slowly waved as their son and brother disappeared down the street. The wind was cold.

During the next days Maria could hardly restore her normal routine. She was constantly filled with thoughts and prayers for her absent son.

After two-and-a-half weeks a letter arrived. George, off-duty that day, quickly brought the unopened letter in to Maria.

Dear Father and Mother:
I have been assigned to the mortar division of the SS
and will be leaving for basic training in warfare.
Right now I'm stationed in Renchen. When you receive this I will probably have three days left to stay
here. I wish I could see you before I have to leave.

Love,
Reinhold

As Maria read the letter, she felt dizzy; her worst fears
had come to pass. She silently handed it to George.

As he read, his face became flushed, and his jaws tightened. "They can't do this! Don't they know Reinhold isn't
even eighteen yet? He stopped for a moment to gather his
thoughts. "The SS[12] has very dangerous assignments. I
don't want my son in that outfit."

"But what can we do?" Maria asked.

"We will go to Stuttgart today and speak to the SS commander. If we catch the next train, we should be able to
reach the headquarters before four o'clock."

The children were home from school that day, and when
Kurt heard of Reinhold's assignment, he seemed almost as
upset as his parents. It did not seem fair that Reinhold, who
had no sympathy for the Nazi cause, should have to risk his
life to such a degree in its defense.

"Don't worry," Kurt assured his parents. "Ruth and I
will take care of Helmut. And I'll call Dr. Wagner and tell
him where Papa is."

"Thank you, Son," Maria replied, as she and George
quickly prepared for the trip. "Please pray for us, too."

As the couple sat in the train, gazing at the countryside,
Maria turned to her husband and said, "I feel as if we're
walking right into the lions' den—I wonder how Daniel
felt." George smiled stiffly as she continued, "I don't think

---

12. "Schutzstaffel"—the black-uniformed special guards of
the Nazi Party.

we've ever faced anything this difficult together, have we, Papa?"

George sat with his hands folded on his lap. "I'm afraid that the lions we're going to face are very hungry."

The train slowed as it neared the outskirts of Stuttgart. Maria's heart began to beat heavily and her palms felt moist and cold. She looked at George's eyes; as a salesman he knew how to look confident, but his eyes could not conceal his apprehension. He nervously glanced at his watch, his thoughts and prayer a jumble in his mind.

If I did not love my son so much, Lord, I wouldn't even dare to do this. I'll probably look back on this time and think I was crazy. But I don't want Reinhold to go to war; I don't want to lose him. You are God, and I'm just a little speck on the earth—yet you care about us and about Reinhold. But if he must go to war, go with him and keep his faith strong. We may lose our son, but I don't want you to lose his soul.

To their relief, the Ziefles had only a short walk from the depot to the SS headquarters. As they neared the doors, George glanced again at his watch—almost four o'clock. Inside, they approached a sergeant seated at a desk. "Sir, we would like to see the commander concerning our son who is stationed at Renchen."

The soldier took their names, then rose and approached an officer at the back of the room. They spoke quietly. The sergeant briskly walked back, sat down at his desk, and without looking up, said flatly, "You may see him at five o'clock. Sit over there."

George thanked him and stepped back to the wooden bench to wait. After sitting still as long as he could, George finally stood and quietly paced the floor. Maria stared at her feet, gripping her gloves tightly.

Just after five, two guards approached them and escorted them into the commander's office. The man made a few quick notes on a pad of paper, then peered at the couple. Benevolence was nowhere on his countenance. "Are you Ziefle?" he barked.

"Yes, sir."

"Whatever you want, get to the point. My time is too valuable for chitchat."

"Sir, first I thank you for giving us your time." George spoke gently, but with confidence. "My son, Reinhold, is being drafted into the SS without my knowledge or permission. He's only seventeen, so he has no business being sent to the fighting front. I request that you release him from the SS."

The officer leaped from his chair, slamming his fist on the desk as he rose. "Are you an idiot?" he shouted. "Do you know what you're asking me to do?"

Maria held George's arms tightly, trying to keep him calm. George remained in control of his emotions as he answered, "We're concerned only about our son. He's not even of age yet, and he still needs us."

The commander glared at the couple and growled, "I should have both of you arrested for this act of treason! What do you think would happen to our national defense if we allowed every soldier to go wherever his mama or papa wanted him, eh? The only way you could possibly have him released is to see Himmler personally."

Himmler, head of the SS, had terrorized Germany. To approach him with such a request would be to face a firing squad. Maria's heart sank in despair. She could feel George droop slightly.

Her eyes already flooding with tears, Maria timidly asked, "May we see Reinhold while he is in Renchen, before he is transferred?"

"The standard visitation time is thirty minutes. You may see him in the morning. Now get going. I have others waiting to see me yet this afternoon."

The couple, hanging their heads, walked out the door and through the main office. Maria pressed her gloves tightly against her mouth to muffle her sobs. George gently put his arm around her and led her toward the train station. The twilight kindly hid their misery from curious eyes. The train ride home seemed twice as long.

The next morning George and Maria drove to the military camp at Renchen. George had received permission to borrow a Red Cross car for the trip. The reunion was not what they had hoped for. They had no privacy, but sat with Reinhold in a large hall bustling with trainees and officers. It was almost impossible to express private thoughts.

Reinhold was as disappointed as his parents about their failure to gain his release, but he tried to accept the inevitable with stoicism.

As their half hour drew to a close, the three sat stiffly in their chairs, glancing at one another uncomfortably. Maria, unable to hold back, finally burst out weeping and bent forward to hold her son in her arms. George and his son stared at each other through the tears welling up in their eyes.

Reinhold spoke, his voice trembling. "Mama, Papa, I will miss you—and I love both of you, and Kurt and Ruth and Helmut, too." He stopped to gather his emotions. "Tell them I miss them, please?"

Maria and George nodded, neither trusting their voices.

Reinhold tried his best to smile as he assured them, "Don't worry; everything will be all right. God will take care of us. True?"

George cast aside his self-consciousness and put both arms around his firstborn. "God be with you, Reinhold." He turned his head to hide the streams of tears. An officer was approaching to announce the end of their half hour. He took his wife's arm and gently pulled her up from her chair. "We must go."

The two slowly moved toward the door, trying to maintain composure. As George pushed the door open, they looked back once more. Reinhold, in his uniform, lifted his hand timidly. His jaw trembling, he whirled and walked the other way.

V

September 1944

Revenge is a judgment which is enjoyed coldly. We know exactly when England will be smashed. Then England will collapse. We will beat it into submission, and to be sure, day after day and night after night.

—Joseph Goebbels

Life was no longer predictable. It almost was safer now to measure time in days, and not even consider months and years. To survive and exist were honorable enough.

Now even the basic food items—flour, sugar, meat and milk—were in short supply, if available. The milk was so watered down it was blue. The Ziefles focused their energies on finding enough to eat. George would repair a farmer's sewing machine in exchange for food. Maria and the children, at harvest time, gleaned the fields, trying to find ears of corn to supplement their meager food supply. They often had to walk a long way to find a field that had not yet been picked clean by other families. The work was slow and tiring and, for a five-year-old like Helmut, the days never went fast enough. But hungry stomachs gave all the incentive needed when there was no food at home.

Ingenuity was the key to having food. To make syrup which she could substitute for sugar, Maria would simmer a kettleful of sugar beets for a week. To insure themselves of eggs and meat, the Ziefles kept a dozen hens in the shed adjoining their house, and several rabbits in cages behind the house. Ruth now had her pets, though for other reasons than companionship!

Fortunately, the Nazis favored large families, so the Ziefles were rewarded with a moderate-sized garden plot about a half-mile from their home. Nothing from the garden was wasted. The greens from the vegetables were fed to the rabbits. That was not enough, however, so Maria often sent Helmut to pick grass along roads and ditches as supplemental feed for the creatures.

There was no way of avoiding the preoccupation with finding food; sometimes even Maria had the sensation that she was living an animal existence, merely trying to survive from one meal to another.

But soon they were to be tested by a new threat. September was almost over. Ruth, busy with studies from her new school in Heilbronn, was specializing in chemistry. Helmut, when not feeling hungry, was occupied with his playmates. Kurt had been accepted by the German Air Force and was eagerly waiting to report that week to flight training school at Kirchheim, Teck.

It was Wednesday night, and George wanted to discuss the future with Kurt. "I suppose you have much to do if you'll be leaving for training on Saturday," he began.

Kurt was studying the instruction sheet that came with his acceptance to the Air Force. "Not really, Papa. About all I have left is to say good-bye to my friends."

Maria interrupted as she glanced up from her needlework, "This house will be so empty with both you and Reinhold gone."

George gazed at Kurt seriously. "Flying—especially in war—is terribly dangerous. Are you really sure that is what you want to do?"

Kurt grinned confidently and leaned back in the sofa. "Oh, Papa, you worry too—"

A horrible explosion shattered the peacefulness and rattled the windows. As if by reflex, George shouted, "To the cellar! I'll get Helmut from the bedroom!" The four were already rushing down the stairs. George dashed into the bedroom to retrieve Helmut. The two arrived in the cellar only seconds behind the rest, Helmut crying loudly from the confusion. Maria took the young boy in her arms.

Kurt was intrigued by the sudden mysterious blast. "What was the explosion from, Papa?"

George thought for a moment. "It could be that one of our planes crashed. If it were an enemy plane, the sirens would be on."

"But we didn't hear any plane before the explosion," Kurt responded.

"Maybe a wine vat blew up!" said Ruth with a giggle. No one else seemed to think it was humorous.

There had been no other explosion for several minutes, and George was becoming more curious. "Kurt, let's go up and try to find out what happened," he said. Kurt eagerly joined him. "We'll be back in a couple of minutes, Maria."

Outside on the street they found Herr Müller and several other men discussing the event. George asked as he approached them, "Does anybody know what that explosion was?"

Müller seemed distraught. "I think it was a bomb planted by an enemy of the Reich—probably a Jew. I hope he is publicly hanged!"

Herr Fischer, another neighbor, commented, "Maybe it is a new weapon which the Allies invented. But if so, how are we going to be safe from a bomb that no one knows is coming?" The group stood in tense silence for moment.

"Well, I don't know about you men, but we're going back to the cellar for a while," George announced. He turned toward the house and Kurt followed.

George entered the cellar and reported, "I don't think—"

"Sh-h-h," Maria whispered. "Helmut is sleeping."

George lowered his voice. "I don't think anyone really knows what the explosion was. Let's stay here, just to be safe. Why don't we get some sleep?''

The four settled down on the straw mattresses. Suddenly another "boom" shook the family to consciousness. This explosion sounded farther away than the first. Still there were no sirens. Fifteen minutes later they heard a faint rustling sound; a third blast splintered the silence—no airplanes, no warning.

"George, we must pray!" Maria pleaded. "We don't know how much danger we're in." He nodded and they all knelt on the dirt floor. The family remained in the cellar the rest of the night.

The following morning George doubled his efforts to find out what had happened. The only facts available were that the explosions came from aerial bombs and that twenty-four people had been killed. Further rumors were abundant.

The people of the city apprehensively went to bed that evening. The Ziefles stayed in the cellar. Their precautions were not in vain. Between 10:30 and 11:00 that night, two more of the mysterious bombs fell on their city.

Many people began commuting to other towns each night rather than endangering themselves in their own homes. The danger was fearsome enough without adding the uncertainty of its origins.

As the rumors gained momentum, the people of the Heilbronn gave a name to their phantom attacker— "Bombenkarle."[13] He was reputed to be a former Jewish resident of the city who had been expelled by the Nazis and was now gaining revenge by hitting selected targets. "Bombenkarle" did not visit on the third night, which only multiplied the people's suspense.

The quiet night was a relief to the Ziefles, but the following day was Kurt's scheduled departure. His anticipation of the new adventure had weakened during the events of the past few days. "I wish I could stay home and help,"

13. "Bombing Charlie."

he confessed as the family ate their breakfast. "This 'Bombenkarle' business worries me."

Maria's sadness at losing another son gained sudden momentum when Kurt voiced his desire to remain home. Her prayers for his soul were having their effect, but soon he would be entering an environment where God was an embarrassment.

Lord, you alone can help him now. It was bad enough when he wanted to go, but now your seed of love is sprouting in his heart. Don't let it die!

Maria rose to get her Bible from the bookshelf. She sat down, opened the Book, and waited for the rest to be silent. Reading solemnly from Psalm 91, "He that dwelleth in the secret place. . ." Maria's selection took on special meaning to the sober little family group.

"Now, Kurt, we are going to pray for God to keep you while you are in the Air Force." To Maria's amazement, Kurt accepted the prayer with enthusiasm. The week's mysterious attacker had made a profound change in his attitude.

The family again made the sad expedition to the streetcar stop. Helmut adored Kurt, and they had often spent time together entertaining each other. Helmut walked beside him that morning, holding his brother's hand tightly. Finally the little fellow blurted, "Please, Kurt, can't I go with you?"

Kurt chuckled at his small partner. "I don't think they allow little boys in the barracks. But don't worry, I'm sure I'll be able to come home and visit you once in a while."

"But who will I play with when you're not here?"

"You play with the other little boys in the neighborhood. Besides, you're five now, and you must learn to take care of yourself."

Helmut was not convinced, but the streetcar was rumbling toward them, so he had no time to argue. George circled Kurt's shoulder with one arm, grabbed his hand and pumped it warmly as he tried to hold back the tears rising in his own eyes. The rest wept freely as they put their arms around him; Helmut took hold of Kurt's legs from behind.

Maria kissed her son. Then gazing into his eyes, she whispered, "You will be in my prayers—every day."

"Thank you, Mama," he replied, his voice quivering. He raised his voice over the loud squeal of the braking streetcar. "I will miss you! I love you all!" He leaped on board and handed his fare to the conductor. The car lurched forward and slowly clattered down the street as the family waved sorrowfully. The familiar sense of loss was no easier the second time than the first. In spite of the beautiful weather, it was a silent and miserable walk home.

"Bombenkarle" visited again that evening, dropping two bombs shortly after eight o'clock. Seven people were killed. The Nazis took full advantage of the rumors, which they had no doubt originated, implying Jewish responsibility for the bombings.

The vicious rumors stirred Maria's heart and called forth memories of her Jewish acquaintances. They had been unceremoniously forced out of their homes for "resettlement" in the east. No one seemed to protest. The incessant propaganda had worked.

Maria wondered what had happened to these people. She had heard nothing about them since they left. Someday she would know.

I wish I knew how to pray for them. They are chosen people—your people, God. But they are treated like criminals. We never hear the whole truth of what the Nazis are doing to them. We suffer for your sake, but I sense their lot is much, much worse. Be merciful to the Nazis, for they do not even realize their insanity; but, dear God, deliver your chosen people!

"Bombenkarle" never struck there again, and the citizens of Heilbronn remained uninformed as to its origin. The Nazi leaders were unwilling to reveal that the Allies had developed a superior weapon—a pilotless plane controlled by ultra-shortwaves. Flying at an altitude of almost 30,000 feet, the airplanes entered German territory undetected, then released their deadly payload eight miles from the target. Fortunately for the people of Heilbronn, the devices had been relatively inaccurate in hitting the railroad center, but the psychological effect of the silent destroyer was quite devastating.

Many people, however, remained oblivious to the mounting danger to Germany itself, still convinced that the Third Reich was invincible. One morning Maria was conversing with her neighbor, Frau Fischer, in front of the Ziefle home. Convinced that Germany was heading for inevitable defeat, Maria carefully expressed her doubts; but Frau Fischer obstinately denied the possibility.

"Frau Ziefle, how can you be so pessimistic?" Her voice hinted of arrogance. "The Führer promises that we will win this war. It won't be long before he will unveil his new miracle weapons; then soon the enemy will be defeated!"

"Only God can give us miracles. He is the only one who can protect us. We must put our trust in Him."

Frau Fischer proudly lifted her chin. "Not me! Hitler is the only one I can trust! Who needs God?" She stared sharply at Maria, pointing her finger as she continued. "If I were you, I'd get rid of such a critical attitude. We don't like people who are not with us one hundred percent. You've put yourself in a dangerous position."

"You think I'm disloyal." Maria's voice was adamant. "I love Germany. I don't want our country to be defeated. I just know that all the troubles we've faced in the last year are signs that we are not as powerful as we thought we were."

"Hmph! Our willpower is strong—we will overcome any obstacles. As long as we are united in love and service to the Führer, nothing can stop us!"

Maria turned toward the front door in an attempt to finish this uncomfortable conversation. "Please excuse me, but I must feed Helmut now. It is already past his lunchtime." She mounted the steps and turned the doorknob.

"Wait and see!" the other woman's shrill voice rang out. "Soon all our enemies will be defeated. Heil Hitler!"

Maria entered and trudged up the stairs. "Miracle weapons!" she muttered. "The Nazis can't even provide us with enough food—and they keep taking our anti-aircraft guns to the front!" She laughed as she wagged her head. "What are *we* supposed to use for miracle weapons to protect Sontheim—cabbages?"

Defense was now a pathetic joke. Only twelve light anti-aircraft guns remained to protect the entire Heilbronn area. Gradually more of the citizens began to sense how vulnerable they really were. Since the "Bombenkarle" scare, the Heilbronn area had not been attacked, but southern German cities were being hit with greater and greater frequency by Allied planes. As winter drew closer, the wailing of the sirens became a daily ordeal; in November, the alarms were sounded 99 times—the Ziefles were running for shelter day and night. Many, wearied of the continued precautions, carelessly ignored the warnings.

The nightly interruptions to her sleep were fatiguing Maria. Helmut was affected even more. The incessant eerie wails of the sirens had made him so nervous that he would run crying to his mother's bed whenever they awakened him.

Because of the increasing threat, the Ziefles were now taking refuge in public shelters which seemed to be safer than their cellar. This made readiness more necessary, so Maria began putting Helmut to bed fully clothed. Often they made use of the underground shelter near the Matthäuskirche; at other times they resorted to open-air sanctuary among the trees along the Deinenbach, a brook on the east side of Sontheim.

When the alarm sounded again on the night of November 24, Maria decided to take Ruth and Helmut to safety along the Deinenbach. The air was cold, but the silvery moonlight offered a beautiful evening to wait outdoors rather than in a stuffy, overcrowded vault. But the unpleasantness of an air raid could not be avoided, and she wished George were there to lead them.

Many other people stood nervously in the darkness. Gloomy shadows from trees and humans aggravated Helmut's uneasiness, and he clung to his mother's legs, shivering and whimpering.

A deep droning sounded in the distance, coming closer and growing louder. Though twenty miles away, the roar of hundreds of enemy bombers was easily recognized. Just south of Heilbronn, signal rockets, intended to confuse the enemy and prevent the city from being struck, exploded brightly in the sky and descended slowly like balloons as they illuminated the countryside below. Helmut, thrilled with the spectacle, began jumping up and down and shouting at each new burst of light.

The southern horizon began to glow with orange light, punctuated by frequent bright bursts; Stuttgart was under attack. "May God have mercy on them," said a man standing nearby. But the nearness of the burning city reminded them all of their own defenseless predicament.

The muffled booming continued as the people watched in awe. Their hearts all wrestled with the same question—when and where would the planes strike next?

VI
December 1944

Supper was almost ready as George trudged up the stairs and into the living room that early December evening. Maria stepped out of the kitchen to greet him. Without removing his coat, he sprawled on the couch and sighed, "I hope we don't have another alarm tonight. That one at 4:30 made five so far today. I was trying to transport those wounded soldiers who arrived on the hospital train, and all the alarms made the job twice as hard. But we finally got them all moved—102 of them. I'm exhausted."

Maria smiled and answered, "I hope you can get some rest, too. And I made your favorite—the pork chops you bought from that farmer the other day." She returned to the kitchen.

"Where are Ruth and Helmut, Maria?"

"They should be back any moment. They went for a walk. Ruth told me that she had wanted to attend the movies with her friends tonight after school, but the teacher kept them so late the movie had already started. Her friends went anyway, but she decided to come on home. I'm glad, because she didn't have permission to go."

Just then the two children entered the house. "Hello, Papa!" they exclaimed.

"Come and eat," Maria's voice called from the kitchen.

Heilbronn and its suburbs were at that moment bustling with people returning from work, shopping, attending the movie theaters, and waiting for trains to take them on trips. The constant air-raid warnings had become a mere inconvenience; living daily with danger and death had calloused their concern.

But as the Ziefles gathered around the supper table and the citizens pursued work and pleasure, a young Russian woman, a captive laborer, returned from work to the home of her houseparents in Heilbronn. Her steps were hurried as she entered the house and quietly descended to the cellar. Puzzled, her hostess went down and confronted her. "What's wrong? What are you doing down here?"

Nervously the girl replied, "Heilbronn will be destroyed tonight. I am staying down here." No one ever discovered how the foreign workers received advanced warning.

George was in the middle of his prayer for the family's supper. The low-pitched growl of sirens coming alive stopped him. He jumped up and went for his coat, filled with fresh vigor in the face of the duties ahead of him. "I'll eat supper when I come back. I've got to go."

Maria called, "Why don't you take two pork chops along and eat them on the way?" She hurried out to him, wrapping the meat in brown paper.

"Thank you, Mama!" He kissed her quickly, then kissed Ruth and Helmut who were donning their wraps. "I'll see you later!" He ran outside and mounted his bicycle. It was 6:55 p.m., December 4.

Maria and the children bustled out the door and into the street. As they hurried down Ackermannstrasse toward the shelter, the full alarm sounded. As the air began vibrating with the thunder of warplanes, the trio quickened their pace in order to reach the larger one at the Matthäuskirche. Rumbling aircraft engines shook the ground beneath their hurried footsteps.

Maria stopped, frozen with fright. Twin engine Mosquitoes were directly over them, their floodlights shining on the street and rooftops. *Lord, if they drop their bombs now we're all dead!*

Helmut cried out, "Jesus! Help us! Please!" Ruth whimpered fearfully.

Maria grabbed the two children's hands and began running. It seemed so futile. They were hopelessly illuminated by the lights as they ran down the street. *God, we need you like never before!*

The street was nearly empty; most people had already found safety. A policeman stood on the sidewalk furiously cranking his portable siren. There was no time to reach the church shelter. The three Ziefles turned into the shelter at the Nöth winery. For some unknown reason, the planes had not yet dropped any bombs. When the night was over, it would be obvious—their target was Heilbronn, not Sontheim. Two hundred and thirty-five Lancaster bombers were flying in columns on either side of Heilbronn. A few miles east of the city they would make the turn that would bring them back to unleash their hellish cargo.

The Nöth wine cellar trembled from the awesome bellowing of the returning Lancasters. Its eighty occupants sat and stood in fearful silence, various emotional responses etched on their faces. Death seemed to be laughing at them. The air-raid warden standing near the large steel doors glanced at his watch in the dim light of battery lanterns—7:15.

The low-flying Mosquito fighters continued to swoop above the buildings. The war-weary Ziefle family, though enclosed in the shelter, could picture in their minds the crackling magnesium illumination bombs, bathing the blacked-out city in a bright greenish glow. A few minutes later the deafening roar of the Lancasters was split by 1150 tons of incendiary bombs and heavy explosives hitting their targets.

In spite of her previous experiences, Maria could hardly believe the ear-splitting roar and the shock of the explosions. People screamed and pointed at the steel doors—with each wave of explosions, they bulged like paper in the wind. All around her people were on their knees crying out to God. One man, hands over his ears, shouted continuously, "God, forgive! Save me! Lord, have mercy on me!"

A woman next to him mumbled softly as she frantically fingered the beads of her rosary.

Others in hysterics clawed at the concrete walls, as if attempting to climb out. Maria stared with helpless compassion at these people who had arrogantly denied the Creator's power.

Helmut, wide-eyed, observed the terror of the people around him. The continual races to the shelter and his innocent faith had finally stiffened his tolerance for these frightening events.

The rumbling of the planes began to recede. It was 7:45 p.m. The still-sporadic explosions would continue all night, for many of the bombs were timed to detonate after impact—by as much as ten hours. But the people in the wine cellar were beginning to calm.

Maria was anxious to go home and find if her house was safe. She also wanted fresh air. But it was the warden's responsibility to decide when they could leave. She remembered a pamphlet the government had issued earlier in the year that informed the citizens they should wait in the air-raid bunkers for up to five hours to insure their safety. She put the warning out of her mind and heard with relief the warden's instructions which allowed them to go.

The group filed outside—and gaped in horror, shielding their eyes. The inner city of Heilbronn was a blinding fireball. Maria pleaded quietly, "Lord, put your angels around George tonight. Don't let that inferno swallow him up. Be merciful to us all."

Holding tightly to Ruth and Helmut's hands, Maria carefully picked her way homeward. As they turned east at Kolpingstrasse, they collided with a staggering mass of smoke-blackened people, fleeing from Heilbronn into Sontheim. It looked like a death march.

A woman ran frantically toward the Ziefles and grabbed
Maria's arm. Her coat was partially burned, and she was
covered with dirt and soot. "Frau, please help me!" she
begged. "My house was hit and the rest of my family was
killed! Please!" Maria did not even ask her name; letting go
of Ruth, she placed her arm behind the woman and led her
toward home—if it indeed was still there.

The four turned off Ackermannstrasse and anxiously
hastened past the Knaus home. Their house was there, and
intact! With thanks in her heart, Maria led her group into
the house. The woman in Maria's arms kept whimpering, "I
want to die too. Why wasn't I killed?"

The four filed upstairs to the kitchen. The unfinished
supper was still on the table. And the coffee was still warm.
Though there was no electricity, the orange glow from the
city provided sufficient light in the room so they could see
each other. Exhausted, they forced themselves to eat. The
stranger finally was able to tell them that her name was
Eva. Her husband, two children, and a cousin were all
killed when a bomb exploded beside their house. Now in
shock, the woman looked blankly around her. Maria led her
to the living room, helped her lie on the couch, and put a
blanket over her. Eva immediately fell into a deep stupor.

Maria sat down again at the kitchen table. "Helmut,
Ruth, let's pray for your papa now. I'm sure he's in great
danger." The three bowed their heads and took turns im-
ploring God to protect their beloved father. Maria added a
plea for their guest in the living room. When finished, they
all prepared for bed.

Lying beneath the quilts, Ruth restlessly thought of all
her classmates who were no doubt in the movie theater
when the planes arrived. "Did they get out? Did they find
shelter? I would have been there without my parents' permission—would God have protected me?" She would not
know until morning.

Fifty miles south at Kirchheim, Teck, two Air Force

trainees were strolling toward the barracks. "Look," one of them said, "is that a fire in the north?"

"Must have been a bombing, Rolf."

"I suppose it must be about twenty miles away. Ludwigsburg, maybe, eh, Kurt?"

"You're probably right. I feel sorry for those people." The two stared at the orange glow for a few seconds, then proceeded into the barracks.

The brilliance of the nearby inferno illuminated her bedroom as Maria attempted to sleep. She wondered about friends and relatives who lived in the vicinity. And she prayed again especially for George.

George had reached the Red Cross station while the planes were still making their first pass over the city. He hurried into the workers' room of the air-raid shelter and sat anxiously waiting for the other ambulance drivers to arrive. He shivered from the vibrations of the airplane engines as he pulled the pork chops from his coat pocket.

A man dashed through the door. It was his partner, Karl Wieland. "Karl!" George exclaimed. "Where are the other drivers?"

Karl stared at him, his eyes big with fear. "No one else has arrived? Some of the men live closer to the station than we do."

"Dr. Wagner, Dr. Baumann and a couple of nurses are here—but that's all. Maybe some of them were too scared to come out."

The drone of the planes was suddenly broken by the staccato of dozens of incendiary bombs clattering like hail on a sheet-metal roof. Deafening blasts shook the bunker; several bombs had fallen very close by. The building shuddered violently. The lights flickered and went out.

Karl cried out in the blackness, "George, I'm afraid to die! Pray for me!"

"Don't worry, Karl, I already have!" George shouted above the roar of the planes and explosions. "God is going to protect us! Be brave—we have a big job to do tonight!"

Five waves of Lancasters unleashed their deadly fury upon the city. George and Karl sat helplessly in the room, wondering if their wives and children were still alive.

The sound of planes thinned into the distance, though the timed explosions continued the destruction. Dr. Wagner, holding a flashlight, came running into the shelter.

"George, Karl, we must get our lights back on. Baumann and I can't give treatment using only flashlights and candles." He sounded desperate. "Do you know how to start the auxiliary generator? Willi isn't here to do it."

George jumped to his feet. "I've never done it before, but I've watched Willi start it several times. I'll run outside and see what I can do."

George hurried upstairs and stepped out into the blazing night. All around him were shattered houses being gutted by flames. He took a few steps toward the vehicle garage where the generator was housed. He stopped in dismay. Flames were pouring from the roof of the building.

George whirled and ran back down to the shelter. Karl and Dr. Wagner were coming up the stairway. "Karl, the garage is on fire! You'll have to help me if we're going to start the generator."

"How bad is the fire?" Karl countered. George ran up the steps and Karl followed him outside. He stared at the blaze. "I'm not going in there with you! I don't want to be a dead hero."

"Karl!" George was angry. "People's lives will depend on the light that generator provides! Some of those people might even be your own family!"

Karl shrugged his shoulders weakly and nodded. George sprinted toward the garage, Karl running close behind. They dashed through the door and peered through the smoke. Every vehicle was destroyed—except theirs.

"Get our ambulance out away from the flames," George barked. "I'll start on the generator. Come back and help me when you're done."

The men separated. George turned up the collar on his jacket and hurtled through a maze of fallen beams and bricks. The generator stood silently in the glow of the flames; it was far enough away from the flames to be safe! He took a deep breath, bent low and ran toward it, the heat tearing at his lungs.

He reached for the controls and pulled the choke. He fumbled for the crank, inserted it, and gave it three violent jerks. Nothing. He frantically ran outside for cool air. Karl was stepping out of the ambulance.

"Karl, come and help me!"

"I'm not going back in that furnace!" he argued.

"Well, then, stand at the door and keep an eye on me. If I need help, you'll be ready."

Karl consented to stand watch at the door.

George dove back into the smoke and rubble, trying to avoid breathing the poisonous air. He reached the generator and grabbed the crank. He whirled it viciously. The engine sputtered; he desperately adjusted the choke. It revived. He closed the switch to the powerline and the generator howled into action.

As George ran back to the building, the first bombing victims staggered toward the Center. They were a frightening lot. Some were covered with wet clothes as protection from the heat. Many shielded their faces with handkerchiefs, hoping to save their lungs from the acrid fumes. Soon over a hundred people had crowded into the waiting room. George and Karl tried to help the injured settle themselves. The ones with the worst burns were laid out on pallets.

Dr. Wagner stepped into the room to survey the work ahead of him. Spotting George he called, "Ziefle, thanks for starting the generator. That will save many lives tonight." George nodded and smiled as the doctor went on, "I think you should start out with the ambulance. Is yours ready?"

George suddenly realized the miracle that had occurred with his vehicle. "All were destroyed except mine, Doctor.

We'll leave right away." He and Karl hurried out the door and toward their van.

George turned the ambulance into the street. Directly in front of them lay a woman. The two jumped out and ran to her side. Her mouth and nose full of ashes, she was gasping for breath. The men quickly cleaned the debris from her air passages and she regained her breath. They helped her into the back of their van and drove to the door of the Center. Their first rescue, and they had hardly left the Red Cross station.

The men drove through the streets slowly, not only to avoid running over the thousands of people fleeing the city but to spot as many victims as possible whom they could help. They stopped and administered first aid wherever there was need.

The streets were now just rubble-strewn alleys between walls of fire. As they turned a corner, the street before them was filled with flames from a collapsed building. Concerned for the people who might be trapped on the other side, George downshifted and accelerated the vehicle, wildly careening through the flaming rubble.

"George! Are you crazy! You'll kill both of us!" Karl cried.

"This isn't a Sunday drive, Karl! People's lives are at stake!" In seconds, they had cleared the scorching maze. "Thank you, Lord!" he whispered.

Before long the ambulance was full and George drove the van as fast as he could to the Red Cross Center. He and Karl unloaded the victims and began their third trip.

This time the men were almost downtown. Hundreds of fires had combined and engulfed the entire area. The glaring heat sent hurricane-like blasts of scorching air among the burning buildings. It seemed impossible that anyone would still be alive in there. Grief welled up in George's heart as he thought of the people, trapped in those once-beautiful buildings, who would be only ashes by morning.

Suddenly a figure stumbled out of the flames toward the ambulance. It was a man with a blanket over his body. The blanket was burning. George opened his door as the man fell almost in front of the van. George and Karl rushed to him and tore the blanket from him. They carefully helped the man into the ambulance. He was badly burned, but he would live.

As they ground to a halt after spotting another victim, a large "thump" sounded from the vehicle's undercarriage. The two paid no attention—the streets were full of debris. As George and Karl bent over the victim, a policeman ran up behind them yelling, "Are you guys trying to get killed? You just drove over a bomb!"

The two men froze and stared at each other. George finally managed a wry smile. "I think we have angels around our ambulance tonight!" Karl nodded weakly.

The van full again, in a matter of minutes the men had unloaded at the Center and were on their way. They threaded their way along a wide boulevard, divided in the center by large trees. But tonight it was a grisly spectacle. People, their clothing ablaze, ran down the street screaming in agony. In desperation many embraced the trees, as if pleading for help, but died as human torches. George anxiously watched for those who could be saved.

The city of Heilbronn flamed and roared like a gigantic blowtorch. Beneath the city thousands cowered, dutifully obeying the government's instructions to remain in the bunkers as long as possible. Several of the shelters were torn open by the suction of the heat and delayed bomb explosions. Flames and poisonous gases swept over the hapless victims and devoured them.

In other shelters, carbon monoxide seeped in and the occupants drowsily suffocated. Some survivors in the bunkers became uneasy, sensing their plight, and attempted to climb out through the narrow escape tunnels. Many such passages were frequently jammed with debris or supplies, and in some instances, the escapees were trapped by the bulk of their own luggage. Those following them were caught in the crush and suffocated.

No place was totally safe. Much of the air-raid shelter at Heilbronn's main hospital as well as its occupants was destroyed. Many wounded soldiers whom George had transferred that morning were killed when their auxiliary hospital was hit.

All the hospitals in the city were demolished. Only two first-aid stations remained—the one on Wilhelmstrasse, and another at the Kaiser-Friedrich-Plaza. That night alone almost 800 people received treatment at the Wilhelmstrasse center for wounds, burns, smoke inhalation and carbon monoxide poisoning. Others, by the next day, had developed heavy infections in the membranes of their eyes, noses, and throats, and also required treatment.

As the sun rose on the following day, George wearily continued the back-breaking but rewarding task. Most of the still-walking victims had left the Center, but now those requiring hospitalization needed transporting. In addition to those from the Red Cross station, hundreds of patients from the Heilbronn hospitals who had survived the bombing needed to be relocated. Many were transferred to the Weissenhof facility by ambulance, horse-drawn wagon, and pushcart. Dozens arrived dead.

Maria arose that morning feeling more tired than when she had gone to bed. George was still not home. The possibility of his being dead clawed at her heart. She could only wait and pray.

Heilbronn had ceased to function as a city. Services, utilities, and businesses were destroyed or crippled. December 4, 1944, had been the worst night in its history. The survivors began the anxious search for the remains of loved ones. Many had been burned beyond recognition or lost in the rubble. Civil and medical records had been devoured by the flames. Eleven years later the count was final: 6,530 dead. More than one thousand were children under ten years of age.

VII
December 5, 1944

*We are completely defenseless. The Reich is grad-
ually being transformed into a complete desert.
Göring is responsible with his Luftwaffe. It is no
longer capable of conducting defensive operations.*

—Joseph Goebbels

The two Air Force trainees at Kirchheim sat noncha-
lantly eating their breakfast in the mess hall. "Say, Ziefle!"
a voice called from an adjoining table. "I heard Heilbronn
was bombed last night. Isn't that where you're from?"

Kurt, ashen-faced, turned to Rolf. Rolf was from Böckingen, another Heilbronn suburb. Their forks fell from their
limp hands. "We've got to go home and check on our families! Let's go see the commander, Rolf." The two scrambled
away from the table and out of the room. They had felt pity
last night when they thought the flames were rising from
Ludwigsburg—now they were filled with near-panic.

Much to their relief, the commander willingly granted
the pair overnight passes. He had heard that the fiery glow
from Heilbronn was witnessed from as far away as Ulm—
nearly 100 miles. He could only advise the two anxious
young men to expect the worst. Tense with the fear of never
seeing their families again, Kurt and Rolf ran to the station
to catch the earliest train home.

Rubbing her eyes and fighting the weariness in her

body, Maria dragged herself upstairs to fix breakfast for her family. Passing through the living room she stepped toward the couch to check on Eva. The blanket was heaped at one end, and there was no one in the room. Maria glanced around. The woman's coat and shoes were not there.

The events of the night had nearly suffocated Maria's spirit, yet concern for the destitute woman welled up in her heart. *God, be merciful to that poor woman. I don't know if she is wandering in the streets or is with friends, but she has lost everything. Somehow, let her sense your love. We may have entertained an angel in our midst.*

Breakfast for the three Ziefles was a simple meal, slow and silent. With Heilbronn in shambles and George's safety in question, there seemed no purpose in hurrying to face the day. Ruth, like her mother, had slept poorly, having spent the night wondering if her schoolmates had escaped the bombing. Helmut was the only one who had energy.

Finally Maria broke the silence. "We really need to find out if your father is all right. I'm wondering if I should take Helmut with me and walk to the Red Cross station this morning." She stared pensively at the window. "But what would happen if the planes attacked again? We might not reach a shelter in time."

Ruth leaned forward in her chair. "Mama, why don't you let me go and find out about Papa? If I rode my bike, I could get there in half the time."

"It's very dangerous for a girl to be alone out there."

"Don't worry, Mama. I'll be careful. Please."

Maria hesitated and then nodded with a slight smile. Ruth jumped from her chair, grabbed her coat and headed for the door.

Reaching the Red Cross Center took much longer than usual. Ruth felt as if she hardly needed a wrap with the heat of the smoldering streets and buildings radiating toward her as she passed. In the city of Heilbronn proper, she found that familiar streets had become craters, and piles of debris often forced her to detour. Several times the stench of burned buildings and charred bodies almost forced her to turn back. The more wreckage she encountered the lower sank her hopes of seeing her father alive.

She finally reached the Red Cross Center, leaned her bicycle against the wall, and ran toward the door. As she stepped inside, a nurse hurried past her. Desperately she grabbed the woman's arm. "Tell me! Is my father still alive?"

The woman, obviously worn from the long night, replied shortly, "Who are you?"

"Ruth Ziefle."

"Oh! You are Herr Ziefle's daughter!" The woman's countenance was suddenly exuberant. "He's still picking up injured people all over the city. Your father is a hero, did you know that, Fräulein? If it were not for him, our Center wouldn't even be operating. He risked his life to start up the generator."

Her anxiety now turned to joy, Ruth asked eagerly, "Will he be able to come home soon?"

"That I can't promise. All of us here are exhausted, and we hope to go home later today. It depends on how soon some others can come to replace us."

"Tell him we're happy that he's all right—and that we love him!" Ruth rushed out the door joyfully.

Wending her way home, Ruth was amazed at how quickly the people of Heilbronn were rallying after the disaster—busily moving rubble, searching for bodies, and attempting to return some sense of normalcy to the city. The job ahead of them was monstrous. Over half of the city's 25,000 buildings were destroyed. Almost all public facilities had been demolished, including the fire stations. Water and gas lines were broken in hundreds of places. Work crews streamed in to help with cleanup and restoration. Some came from as far away as the Ruhr Valley, 300 miles to the northwest.

But peace had not yet returned. Allied planes were relentlessly attacking German targets, trying to force the

Reich to its knees. Though Heilbronn, for the time being, was quiet, other areas were not. Kurt and Rolf's train, nearing Ludwigsburg, was pursued by fighter bombers. Fortunately, the train was entering a tunnel, and the quick-thinking engineer brought the train to a halt once it was inside the mountain.

The bombers, however, blasted the other end of the tunnel, sealing it shut. Unwilling to turn back, Kurt and Rolf walked ten miles to Bietigheim, the next station from which they could reach Heilbronn. Here they encountered several people who had just arrived from there. To Kurt and Rolf's relief, the people assured them that only Heilbronn proper, not the suburbs, was hit during the raid. Their spirits lifted, the two waited impatiently for the train to arrive.

Hoping to avoid the long winding route she had taken to the Center, Ruth attempted to bicycle home in another direction. As she approached her turn off the Allee, she noticed several people working hard with objects on the ground some distance ahead. Instead of making the turn, she approached the scene, curious. When she was able to see clearly the activity, she jerked to a halt, feeling ready to faint. Spread across a large open lot were hundreds of charred, shrunken corpses. For a moment she was so weak she could not even turn away.

"Fräulein, you'd better get away from here. This is no place for you to be!" said a policeman as he waved her away.

Weakly she replied, "I don't think I want to stay. But, sir, could you tell me what happened to the people in the movie theater over in the next block? Some of my classmates were there last night."

The officer hesitated, then gazed at her sadly. "Three hundred people were in there. No one got out alive."

Ruth gasped and cupped her hands over her face. Tears rose quickly in her eyes.

"I'm sorry." The man's voice was tender despite his obvious hurry. "Please, you have to run along. I can't allow unauthorized people to stay around here."

Ruth could hardly see through her tears as she turned her bicycle and pedaled away, her emotions in conflict. She hurried home, bearing news of joy and tragedy.

It was nearly time for supper when George finally came home to rest for the night. As he ate his meal he spoke little of his tireless efforts to save many lives. He was more concerned for the plight of the wounded, homeless, widowed and orphaned. As Maria observed her husband, she tried to remember the dark-haired, vigorous man he was before the war. The gray hair and the lines in his face were only outward indications of the toll the war had taken. She was certain he would never be the same man after the last twenty-four hours. He had seen death as few men ever had.

As the four finished their thin gruel, Maria announced, "Because Papa needs to get his rest, we will have Dämmerstündle now rather than later." She looked at her youngest. "Helmut, which Bible story would you like to hear tonight?"

Helmut brightened with importance and readied his answer. But the closing of the front door and the sound of footsteps stole the family's attention. They looked at each other, puzzled.

George rose from his chair and stepped toward the stairway. "Who's there?" he called apprehensively.

"It's me!" a voice rang back.

"Kurt!" the family chorused. The three at the table sprang to their feet and joined George and Kurt in happy embraces.

With their arms around her son, Maria cried out inwardly, *Why are we allowed such joy when others are left with nothing? Why, Lord, have we been spared?*

VIII
January 1945

We shall never capitulate.

—Adolf Hitler

Fighter bombers were approaching Sontheim in broad daylight. "Hurry, Frau Krauter!" Kurt yelled as they ran frantically across an open field about two hundred yards from home. They were almost to the brook, the Deinenbach. The roar of the attackers was nearly above them.

Suddenly the whistle of released bombs shrieked through the air, and Kurt dove into the grass; his elderly neighbor ran on. The deafening blasts surrounded him. Kurt cautiously raised himself up for a moment. He was hurled to the ground by a hard blow on his right arm. At first he felt nothing. Turning his head he checked himself; shrapnel had demolished his upper arm.

He needed cover, so he jumped to his feet and ran for the brook. He would have to jump across the water to reach the protection of the trees and bushes. Holding his arm with his left hand, he approached the water at full speed and leaped. His feet slipped on the wet ground and he landed in the middle of the brook, his full weight on his injured arm. The suffocating pain obliterated any sensation of January cold from the water.

Kurt looked again at his arm. The mangled, bleeding limb hung loosely, connected to his shoulder only by flesh. His face turned white. "Lord! Have mercy on me!" he cried aloud. The pain increased, but a new sense of peace came over him as he realized that God was hearing his call for help.

His arm and shoulder throbbing with pain, Kurt groped to his feet and stumbled through the brook to one of the hollowed-out shelters along the bank. Herr Ritter, an acquaintance of Kurt, approached him, having noticed the youth grimacing with pain.

"What happened to you, Kurt?" he asked, shocked as he saw the mangled arm.

"Shrapnel!" Kurt gasped. "Can you do anything for it until I get to a doctor?"

In lieu of medical supplies, the man drew a large handkerchief from his pocket and wrapped it around the open wound. He then made Kurt sit down until the bomb attack subsided.

As soon as the planes began to fly away from the town, Herr Ritter helped Kurt to his feet and walked him to Ackermannstrasse. Every movement was torture; Kurt groaned and clenched his jaws as the burning pain tore through him.

Kurt had been home on a two-day pass because his unit would soon be transferred to Czechoslovakia. The war effort was becoming increasingly frantic. The Allies had invaded France in June of the previous year and had occupied Paris at the end of August. Even the rocket attacks against England were not deterring the effort to strangle the Nazi war machine. Kurt had been fortunate to get the pass at all.

It was almost noon of Kurt's first day home when the air-raid sirens had begun to howl. Maria had been at the stove making pancakes for lunch. The family members scrambled for their coats—all except Kurt, who wanted to enjoy every moment he had of his short stay at home.

Scoffing at the danger, Kurt insisted, "Let's not waste these pancakes, Mama. If we take them off the heat now, they'll never taste as good. You go on to the shelter and I'll finish them."

"Kurt, it's not safe!" his father scolded.

"I can take care of myself, Papa. I'll go to the cellar if it gets too bad."

His parents helplessly shrugged their shoulders. Ruth grabbed the suitcase with their important belongings and hurried for the door. Helmut jumped on George's back, and Maria took her husband's arm—her phlebitis had made walking increasingly difficult.

As the Ziefles breathlessly rushed to the shelter, their neighbor with whom they shared the cellar, Frau Krauter, had run into the Ziefle kitchen. Kurt was calmly turning pancakes.

"Kurt, I don't want to stay here and die!" she exclaimed, her face pale with fright. "Please go with me to the Deinenbach where it's safer."

Kurt smiled at the distraught woman. "Frau Krauter, I don't think it will be so bad. Besides, I'd rather stay right here."

Frantic, she pulled on Kurt's sleeve. "Please, go with me!" Out of compassion for the woman, Kurt accompanied her toward the edge of town. Then the airplanes had come. The house would have been safer.

Beneath the ground in their bunker, George and Maria restlessly waited for the all-clear. Anxiety over Kurt nagged at both of them. Unable to sit any longer, George finally turned to his wife. "I have a feeling that something has happened to Kurt. You three stay here and I'll see if I can find him." He rose and hurried out of the shelter.

As George reached Ackermannstrasse his fears were confirmed. Coming from the other direction was Kurt, holding his limp arm, his face white and twisted with pain. George ran to his son and immediately examined the arm; he exclaimed, "I've hardly ever seen such a bad fracture. Let's get you to Dr. Schramm's."

The two walked as fast as Kurt could manage. Approaching the doctor's house, they halted in dismay. The house and yard were filled with others who had been injured in the attack.

"We can't wait that long," George said. "I'll take you to the Red Cross station. Staff surgeon Beck is on duty, and he'll help you."

"But how will we get to Heilbronn?" Kurt asked between clenched teeth.

"I wish we still had our car," George muttered. "And I don't have my ambulance at home. You sit here and wait," he ordered. "I'll go get my bicycle." He ran down the street, and in a few minutes he returned, pedaling furiously.

"You sit on the seat and I'll sit on the bar and pedal," he said to his son.

Kurt swung his leg over the back wheel and tried to perch himself on the saddle. Without any place to rest his feet, balance was impossible. "Papa, this will never work," he insisted. "Let me ride the bike myself."

George steadied the bike while Kurt positioned himself. Summoning all his remaining strength, Kurt held the handlebar with his good arm, pushed on the pedals and moved away. His father ran behind him the entire mile-and-a-half.

At the Red Cross station, Dr. Beck was amazed that Kurt had traveled so far with such an extensive fracture. Concerned that the arm needed immediate treatment, the physician did not even administer anesthesia, but set the arm while Kurt bravely gritted his teeth and George held onto him. With the arm splinted, Kurt could now be transported to Weissenhof where necessary surgery could be done. With George's ambulance nearby, the trip would be comparatively simple.

As George and Kurt left Heilbronn in the ambulance, Maria, Ruth and Helmut arrived back at their home. Stepping inside they all sniffed, puzzled at the burning smell. Ruth ran upstairs. Soon her laughter rang from the kitchen.

"What is so funny?" Maria called as she and her son came into the room.

"Look what Kurt left!" Ruth replied, giggling. Seven black pancakes lay on the still-hot stove. Maria shook her head, wondering what had happened to Kurt.

In a few minutes Frau Krauter came to the house and explained to Maria about Kurt's accident.

Meanwhile, Kurt arrived at the hospital and was hurried into surgery. The fracture was so severe that a long metal pin was required to hold the bone together. George patiently waited for his son to gain consciousness after the operation, then went home.

Maria was overjoyed to hear that the surgery was successful. Though it was not a pleasant event, it was still good to realize that Kurt would be delayed in returning to military duty. If only Reinhold could be home as well.

The following day was Sunday, and Maria sent Helmut with Ursula, a neighbor girl, to the nursery school at the Matthäuskirche. Maria and Ruth would join him later at the morning service. George was on Red Cross duty.

It was almost 10 o'clock and the children's class was getting under way when the sirens began to wail. Frantically the woman in charge searched for the keys to the interior of the church, since the classroom offered little protection.

The planes were overhead already, and the frightened children cowered against a wall. Many were crying. Trying her best to calm the group, the sister had them bow their heads, then gave a short prayer. She looked up and asked, "Can any of you also pray for us?"

Helmut cautiously raised his hand, then lifted his voice. "Lord, don't let those planes hurt us. And bring us home safely. Amen."

"Thank you, Helmut." She noted the quiet confidence in his large brown eyes. "Would anyone else like to pray?" None volunteered.

The church was spared from the attack. But in two days' time over 160 people were killed in the Heilbronn area.

As Kurt lay in the hospital, not only his body was re-

covering, but an astounding change had come over his attitude. George and Maria were delighted when they visited
their son to find him reading his Bible, singing hymns, and
telling his ten roommates about his experience with God.
The Almighty had responded to Kurt's helpless cry as he
lay in agony in the cold water of the Deinenbach. God's
peace had filled his heart in spite of the pain in his body.
This ardent young disciple of the Nazi cause no longer followed the swastika.

Impressed by the encouraging effect Kurt had on his fellow roommates, one of the nurses suggested he expand his
"ministry" to some of the other patients. Before long he was
reading the Bible, praying, and singing for the patients in
seven rooms.

But even a hospital was not free from the anti-God men-
tality of Naziism. One day as Kurt was singing to some patients, an angry voice growled from behind him, "What's
going on in here?"

Kurt turned and looked into the icy eyes of the head
physician. "I just wanted to encourage my friends with the
Word of God and a few hymns," he replied innocently.

"You are disturbing my patients! Get out and don't do
this again!" The patients were as disappointed as Kurt.
But he had made a strong impression on them, and they did
not forget.

A few days later, another air-raid alarm sounded, and
the patients were rushed to the cellar. The patients were so
disquieted that a nurse finally called for Kurt to come and
calm them by praying with them.

Eight days had passed since Kurt's injury. Tomorrow
would be Monday, and Maria lay sleepless in her bed, wondering what the week would bring and praying for her family. It was almost midnight.

"Mother!" a voice whispered loudly from outside the
window. Someone was knocking on the shutters. "Mother!
It's me, Reinhold!"

"Reinhold!" she cried. "I'll be right there!" She shook her husband. "George! Reinhold is outside! Go tell the children!" Maria rose from the bed and hurried to unlatch the door.

She pushed the door open and peered at her eldest. His ruddy face was barely visible in the darkness. She flung her arms around him. "Why are you here?" she said softly. "Is something wrong?"

By now the rest of the family was coming toward the door. Reinhold stepped aside and embraced each one. "I can't stay long. I have to catch up with my unit as fast as I can."

"Mama, make him something to eat," George said, smiling at his eldest.

"What would you like?" asked Maria.

Reinhold thought a moment. "How about bean stew?"

"I'll fix it right away," his mother assured. "Come up to the kitchen so we can talk."

"How did you get here?" George asked as they walked up the steps.

"My regiment is being transferred from the Western Front to the Eastern Front," he began. "At Bietigheim I found out that our train would not go through Heilbronn as planned. I wanted to come home, so I waited in the bathroom at the station until the train began to pull away. Then I ran out and chased it, even though I knew I wouldn't catch it.

"I approached a station official who had seen me running after the train, and asked for an affidavit. Then I was able to get permission to catch up with my unit via Heilbronn. I got on the next train and jumped off in Böckingen and ran all the way here. I'm lucky no one caught me.

"I'll have to leave early in the morning to be able to rejoin my unit. If I'm late I could be shot on the spot as a deserter."

"How about hiding here?" George suggested. "I'm sure it won't be long before the war is over."

"It's too dangerous, Papa. If I were caught here, we would all be shot."

"You're right," George muttered. "There are too many Nazis in the neighborhood."

Maria quietly stood by the stove, stirring the beans. *Lord, why must he be put in such a predicament? If he stays here he will be killed, and if he goes to the Eastern Front...*

Maria steeled herself to stop the tears welling up in her eyes. *I must be strong. I want Reinhold's few hours with us to be happy. God help me!*

George began updating Reinhold about Kurt and his change of heart. Reinhold could hardly contain his joy at the good news. Maria ladled the steaming beans into a bowl and laid it before Reinhold. Forcing a smile she said, "Enjoy it. Eat as much as you can."

Reinhold attacked the food with his spoon. Not waiting till he swallowed, he exclaimed, "This is so good, Mama! You know, I haven't eaten since breakfast?" He continued devouring the stew, then handed the empty bowl to his mother.

She smiled and filled it again. Maria glanced at Reinhold's coat which he had tossed on the chair next to him. Puzzled, she picked it up. "What happened to your coat? It looks like a sieve!"

He put down his spoon and grinned. "Thank the Lord it was the coat and not me! Right after we left Strassburg this evening our train was attacked by enemy planes. We all ran out and hid in the forest, but I forgot to take my coat. There are over forty bullet holes in it."

Maria held the shredded coat to her breast. Her eyes glistened and her lips trembled as she whispered, "Lord, you *are* taking care of us!"

She paused several seconds to calm herself. "Is there anything else you wish while you're here, Reinhold?"

"Mama, could we have a Dämmerstündle? I've been dreaming about it ever since I left home."

"Of course!" Maria replied as she pulled the Bible off the shelf and laid it next to her husband. "But we must be careful to not wake any neighbors. We don't want to arouse any suspicion that you are here."

George opened the Scriptures and read a chapter. Then each one prayed. Emotions peaked as they implored God to protect their son and brother as he went to the Russian Front. A reassuring Presence filled the room.

"Could you sing some hymns, Mama?" Reinhold begged as the prayers came to a close.

"I'll try." Her voice shaky, Maria wistfully sang the melodies that Reinhold often requested as a child. The satisfied glow on his face lifted her spirits.

It was already two a.m. and Maria's voice was getting raspy. "That is enough," she conceded. "We must all get some sleep—but this has been wonderful!"

The family nodded their heads enthusiastically.

"Will you wake me at five, Mama? Maybe Papa and I could visit Kurt at the hospital before I get on the train."

Five o'clock came all too soon, but Maria forced herself from the bed and shook George to consciousness. She slipped her robe on and trudged up the stairs to the attic. She shook Reinhold gently and whispered his name. He opened his eyes and quickly rose. Military discipline had tempered him.

Returning to the kitchen, Maria took paper and wrapped bread and some sausage for Reinhold to eat. When Reinhold entered the kitchen, his father was waiting for him.

Maria let her tears have their way as she put her arms around her son and held him tightly. "God is with you, Son," she whispered.

"He is, Mama. I know He is," Reinhold replied, his cheeks shining with his tears.

They parted and George and Reinhold hurried out of the kitchen. Rubbing their eyes and yawning, Ruth and Helmut came stumbling up the stairs. Reinhold ran down to meet them, and embraced both at once. With innocent faith Helmut declared, "We will see you again soon, Reinhold, won't we?"

"I hope you're right, little brother," he replied with a grin.

Fortunately George had brought his ambulance home the previous evening, so he and Reinhold had no trouble getting to Weissenhof quickly. When they entered Kurt's room he was still sleeping.

Reinhold tapped his brother's shoulder. Kurt muttered and slowly opened one eye. "Reinhold!" he gasped as he jerked up to a sitting position. "What are you doing here?"

Reinhold smiled and put his arm around him. "It's a long story, and I don't have time to tell you. Ask Papa later." He surveyed Kurt's arm. "You are lucky."

"Lucky? No one ever told me that before! Why?"

"I wish my arm were broken now so I wouldn't have to return to the Russian Front. I'm really afraid."

"Why don't you hide?" Kurt whispered.

"That's too dangerous. Say, tell me about what has happened to your life. Papa told me the good news that God has changed your heart!"

"He is right!" Kurt replied with a grin. "If I hadn't fallen into the Deinenbach with my arm smashed to pieces, I might still be convinced that Hitler is the answer to the world's problems. Now I'm sure that he is the cause of this mess we're in right now. Jesus is the only person who can change the world."

They talked quickly; their time was running out. Tearfully the brothers held each other, then separated. The Russian Front would wait no longer.

IX
April 1, 1945

*Let God arise, let his enemies be scattered; let them
also that hate him flee before him.*

—Psalm 68:1

"I want to take you and the children to Maubach tomorrow morning," George announced as he took off his jacket.
He had just arrived for lunch, looking very agitated.

Maria turned toward him, dazed with surprise. "You
are joking, yes?"

"Of course not! Is this any time to joke, with the Americans' guns so close we can hear them? I have to leave Sontheim. The army has ordered the Red Cross and all security
personnel to evacuate by eight o'clock tomorrow morning.
That's why I want you to go; I don't want you living here
without me. Dr. Wagner gave me permission to take you in
my ambulance to Christian and Berta's home tonight before my unit leaves."

Maria looked puzzled. "Where will *you* go?" She stared
at George, then glanced at Ruth and Helmut as they sat
down at the table.

"I have to haul Nazi records farther south and dispose of
them. I think they contain blacklists of people the Nazis
would have punished if they'd won the war. It's almost
funny—I'm sure our name is on at least one of those lists!
When I finish that job, I hope they'll allow me to return to
you." He looked at his wife. "How about it, Maria? Will
you go to the Haiers?"

"I would certainly like to." She turned toward her children. "What do you think, Ruth and Helmut?"

Helmut almost jumped with excitement. "I want to go see Aunt Berta. Please? I don't like air raids."

Ruth had been sitting, quiet and pensive. She stiffened, then blurted, "I want to stay home." She shrugged her shoulders. "Sooner or later, the Americans will be in Maubach, too."

Surprised at her reluctance, George asked, "But don't you think you would be much safer in Maubach?"

"If we have survived all these air raids, we can make it through a few more days or weeks."

"George, have you mentioned this to Kurt yet?" Maria asked.

"I haven't had time. I plan to see him this afternoon, though."

Maria ladled the thin soup into bowls and passed them out. "I'm sorry but this was all the food I dared to use for this meal." She gave a quick smile. "But let's thank the Lord for what we do have, shall we?" The family bowed their heads as George hurriedly prayed.

"I'll be so glad to get away from the noise and the killing," George began as he spooned his soup. "This whole city has gone crazy. I just heard that Karl D'Angelo, the Heilbronn police chief, fled the city a few days ago. He tried to go to Worms, but as he crossed the Rhinebridge, an explosion killed him and his driver.

"And with the airplanes attacking every day now, there are so many wounded people that the hospitals don't even have room. Karl and I have to leave the victims at the hospital doors and drive off—otherwise they won't admit them. And now the planes don't even honor the red crosses on our ambulances—we were almost killed yesterday as we drove through the city! The world has gone mad, I think!"

Ruth looked up from her food. "I think the Nazis are the craziest ones! I saw Herr Schmidt and Herr Müller give the Nazi salute to each other on the street this morning." She shook her head in chagrin. "The way they act, you'd think they were actually winning the war!"

Maria interrupted. "And they act like we 'little people' don't even exist. The Nazis eat white bread, butter, eggs and meat and drink wine—while we stand in line for hours for a cup of sugar and two fish."

"I'm home!" a voice rang up the stairs as the door banged shut.

"Kurt!" the family chorused. They hurried from the table to greet him.

Kurt tramped into the living room carrying a small satchel with his belongings. The large cast in the sling bulged beneath his coat. He grinned as Maria wrapped her arms around him. She quickly steered him to the table, followed by the others, and served him some soup. Helmut proudly sat next to his brother, curiously examining the cast and sling.

"The Americans must be very close to Heilbronn," Kurt commented. "The hospital released all the patients who could walk. They were frantic to get us out of there."

"They're less than 50 miles away," George answered. "Things are coming to an end awfully fast; you couldn't have come home at a better time. I have permission to take our family to Maubach immediately. Because I'm in the Red Cross I have to be out of town tomorrow morning by eight o'clock—I'm going south; after that, Heilbronn will be closed off. Would you like to go to the Haiers, Kurt?"

Kurt thought a moment. "Asking Christian and Berta to take care of four extra people would be too much. They'll be busy now, with the blacksmith shop and the farm. I'd rather stay here."

Ruth excitedly nodded her agreement. Helmut sank down in his chair, dejected. "Kurt, I wanted you to come along so we could play together."

Kurt smiled and ruffled his little brother's hair. "Besides, I think it's important that someone stay here and look after the house."

"That is probably a good idea," George conceded after a moment. "Kurt and Ruth will stay. Mama, I will take you and Helmut at midnight. That's the safest time to travel." He glanced at his watch. "I must hurry back to work. We'll talk more tonight before we leave." He hurriedly donned his jacket and left the house.

Supper that evening was a nervous affair. George discussed with Kurt and Ruth the details of their stay in Sontheim. They would need money for food. With communications in shambles, there could be no pre-arranged manner of sending news to each other.

There were unspoken but unpleasant questions. If there were heavy shelling, would their house be harmed? With George leaving, their family would be split in four directions—would they see each other again? And this would be Ruth's first experience away from her parents. George and Maria treasured their only daughter; she would be so close to the battle. At least with the family in so many places, the chances of some surviving were greater.

There was time for one more Dämmerstündle while they were still at the table. They were especially attentive to Maria's Bible story that night—even restless Helmut. And Kurt's bright-eyed intensity lifted Maria's spirit; she could well remember his aloof manner only months earlier. Each then prayed. They voiced deep-felt concerns—for one another, for their absent Reinhold, for nearby relatives such as Wilhelm and Paula, for friends and neighbors, for their country.

But the unutterable concerns of a mother's heart could only be lifted to heaven by the groans of her spirit. These were the loves of Maria's life: the man who cared for her and returned her devotions, the children who were conceived in her womb and fed at her breast. And the futures of all of them could be controlled by only One.

Midnight came quickly. Helmut was led sleepily from his bed to the ambulance. Kurt and George loaded the bags in the back. Their farewells were brief, each embracing the other. The darkness veiled their tears.

Kurt sniffed loudly, then spoke. "We're never really apart, are we? Not with Jesus in our hearts!"

Maria took his hand and squeezed it. "Kurt, your new faith in God makes this parting so much easier. And I will keep praying for you and Ruth." George started the motor and Maria stepped into the vehicle, lifting Helmut in ahead of her. She pulled the door shut and the van lumbered out into the darkened street.

The clattering growl of the engine made talk difficult, but Maria's heart spoke clearly. *You have protected us this far, Father. From what we have heard, Reinhold is still all right. But we are losing this war, which means many soldiers are being killed. Are you going to keep him safe any longer? I don't know where George will be or how much danger he will encounter. And Kurt and Ruth—I wish I were young and brave again. Without your protection, we won't all see each other again; we are at your mercy, Lord. But thank you that heaven awaits us, no matter what happens.*

It was now April 2—Helmut's sixth birthday. He would spend the day in peaceful surroundings, something he had nearly forgotten, but with only his mother and aunt and uncle to celebrate with him.

He woke early that morning, despite his late-night trip. As he began to dress, he stopped abruptly and sniffed. The house was filled with exotic smells. From the first-floor blacksmith shop came the acrid fumes of the coal forge and the strong scent of horses being shod. The pigs and hens in the adjoining barn added to the scent. But most intriguing was the tangy odor of smoked meat and homemade sausage hanging in the cellar.

He hurried downstairs and into the kitchen. Aunt Berta was standing over the stove. On the griddle, eggs and potatoes sizzled. Helmut's eyes grew wide at the sight.

Berta looked up. "*Guten Morgen*, Helmut! Happy birthday! Did you sleep well?" Her smile made her full, ruddy cheeks look even bigger. She was a strong-looking woman, who worked hard and faced her lot in life with a vigorous faith. Helmut felt secure with her.

Christian, the large and muscular blacksmith, was already at work in the shop below. The clanking of his hammer rang through the floor. He was a quiet man, known more for his excellent repairs than for his conversation.

The little village was delightfully quiet. It seemed like paradise to Maria and Helmut after the winter of violence in Sontheim. The meadows around Maubach were regaining their green. Here there were no planes dropping bombs, no sirens moaning in the night. The only sign of war was the absence of young men, many having been drafted to the fighting fronts. Christian and Berta prayed and wondered daily about their two sons, Gerhard and Hans, who also had gone to war.

Life was not so serene for Kurt and Ruth as they braced themselves for the turbulent days before them. The American guns were now in range of the Heilbronn area and began pounding the city with their destruction. Aside from stepping out for fresh air and to feed the chickens, Kurt and Ruth spent much of their time in the house. They slept in the cellar at night. The rumble of exploding ammunition had become so commonplace that they hardly noticed unless a shell hit close enough to catch their attention.

After two days, the explosions subsided. Sensing that the lull might be only temporary, Kurt hurried to the bakery, hoping to buy some bread. His promptness was rewarded. Not only did he reach the bakery early enough to avoid a long line, but he also received a loaf of bread; there was never a guarantee of enough for every customer. Once home with the bread, he decided it would be advantageous to buy some other food as well. He headed out again in search of a store that might still have food available.

Not relishing the idea of standing in a long line by himself, he stopped at the home of Walter Weller, another wounded soldier like himself. Walter was eager to go along.

Together they hurried down the street.

Several gunshots rang out nearby; the two youths halted and stared about them. They gave each other a puzzled glance.

"Let's go see what happened," Kurt suggested. "It sounds like the shots came from near the Matthäuskirche." The two walked briskly toward the church, which was little more than a hundred yards away. They turned a corner. Up ahead in the street loomed a large anti-tank obstacle, made of several rows of large timbers imbedded in the pavement. In front of the barricade lay a corpse, its head soaked with blood. As the two approached the sickening sight, they could read the sign wrapped around the body: "I was shot as a war criminal." It was the body of Taubenberger, the Nazi branch leader of Sontheim, in front of his own house. Perplexed by the matter, the two youths returned to their original errand. Nearby, a man was boarding up the windows of his house.

"What happened to Herr Taubenberger, sir?" Kurt asked.

The man looked down from his ladder and shook his head. His voice was somber. "When he discovered the barricade in front of his house, he got upset because the American tanks might damage his house. Some women were working on the street, so he ordered them to take their team of horses and pull the timbers out of the ground.

"But then District Leader Drauz came by. When he saw what was happening, he was furious. Then he asked whose idea it was. They told him; so he had Taubenberger arrested and taken to the city hall." He paused. "A few minutes ago, Drauz's bodyguard brought Taubenberger back here and shot him."

Dismayed, Kurt and Walter proceeded toward the Lichdi grocery store on Hauptstrasse; they had heard from others that it was one of the few stores in the town with food still available. When they reached the store, they took their places at the end of the long line. They peered anxiously at the customers leaving the store. Their suspicions were correct; each carried only a small package. It seemed useless to wait an hour for so little food, but survival depended on it.

An angry voice rang out from the store and everyone in line strained his ear to listen. ". . . and anyone who tries to hinder our cause as Herr Taubenberger did will also be shot as a traitor! Don't forget it!" In a few seconds a stout man in a uniform stamped out of the store. It was District Leader Drauz.

Finally in the store, Kurt received his ration—two pounds of flour, a small package of salt, and three sausages. He stared disgustedly at the meager rations, then paid the clerk. As he left the store with Walter, his mind went back to Taubenberger's execution. Kurt was astonished at the insanity of the act—yet it only reflected the chaos that enveloped the entire nation. "Even the Nazis are not loyal to the party," he thought. "They're all interested in themselves. And to think I wanted to fight for their 'new order.' "

By the next day, the guns were in firing range of Sontheim, and shells began hitting the once-peaceful suburb. During a lull, Ruth went out for a short walk. Soon she came running back to the house. "Kurt, I just saw Else, and she wants us to come and stay with her. She seems awfully frightened." Else Ellinger was a good friend of Ruth's, and her family owned a small grocery store near the Ziefle home. Her mother had died in January, and now her father was at the front, leaving Else by herself.

Kurt brightened. "Our hens laid some eggs today. I'll bet Else has enough things left in her store so we could bake oatmeal cookies." He fetched the eggs, then hurried with Ruth to the store a block-and-a-half away.

Else was overjoyed to see the pair, but Kurt could think only of food. "I brought a few eggs," he announced. "Do you have any oatmeal and sugar left so we can make oatmeal cookies?"

"We're in luck, Kurt," she replied. "I still have two pounds of oatmeal and a half-pound of sugar." The three scurried into the kitchen and busied themselves with the ingredients.

Just as Ruth began mixing the batter, a loud explosion shook the floor. Wide-eyed, the three youths waited for something else to happen. All they heard were the blasts in the distance. They ran outside to see what had been hit. They looked around, but no buildings seemed to be damaged.

Kurt glanced up at the 260-foot smoke stack on the Ackermann yarn factory. "Look!" he pointed with his good arm. "A shell went right through the Ackermann chimney! It looks like it could fall any minute."

Fairly immune to danger at this point, the trio finished the cookies and spent the night at Else's, wondering what they should do. The next morning they sought refuge farther away. Finally they found shelter in the Lenz home on Staufenbergstrasse; there were already 24 people crowded into the cellar. Among them were three couples from the Ziefles' neighborhood—Krauters, Ulmers, and Ingelfingers. Life here would be uncomfortable, at best; there were only garden benches to sleep on, the upstairs bathroom was dangerous to use because of the increased shelling, the water was becoming scarce.

The greatest problem for the 27 huddled together in the Lenz's cellar was food. Someone had to go out each day and find more to eat. By now only two bakers in Sontheim were still making bread for the general public; Herr Bord on Staufenbergstrasse and Herr Kraft on Hauptstrasse had moved their ovens to their cellars and continued baking as long as they had ingredients. They of course could not deliver, so customers had to come and pick up their bread.

This created an extra challenge for the group in the Lenz home; of the 23 adults, there were only 4 men to make the trip. But Herr Krauter was too old and weak. And Herr Ulmer was impossible; a short man, he compensated for his stature by bragging that he could shoot down enemy planes with only a rifle. Only Kurt and Herr Ingelfinger were willing and strong enough to bring bread from the bakeries and water from the Deinenbach.

As the group was eating supper the evening Kurt and Ruth arrived, Ingelfinger turned to Ulmer and said, "It's your turn to get food tomorrow." His voice was firm. "I did it today, and you promised to do it tomorrow."

Ulmer flushed. "I-I'm not leaving this house for anything. Do you expect me to go out in those streets and be killed?"

"Ulmer, aren't you ashamed of showing such cowardice in front of all these women?" He glared at the short man. "In that case, I'll get it myself."

Kurt interjected, "Let me go. I'm not afraid."

Ingelfinger flashed an approving glance. "No, Kurt, you just came today and brought some food with you. You go the next day." Kurt nodded.

Suddenly there was a loud crash upstairs, and then the cellar shuddered as a shell exploded nearby. In stunned silence, the people sat wide-eyed for a few moments. Someone came clattering down the stairs—one of the women had been in the bathroom during the explosion. The sight of her racing into the cellar, pulling her clothes back on raised a ripple of nervous giggles in the tension-filled room.

"Let's see what happened, Kurt," Ingelfinger called as he hurried toward the stairs. The two stepped out of the house into the evening twilight. They gawked at their shattered chimney, then at the demolished house on the chicken farm next door.

"That was close!" Kurt gasped. "A few feet less and we might all have been killed."

Ingelfinger scratched his grizzled cheek. "I'll bet some chickens were killed by that shell. There's no one living there right now, and we could use some soup!" The two searched and found two dead hens. They returned to the cellar triumphantly.

Late the next afternoon, Ingelfinger set out to fetch bread and water. "Don't worry if I'm a little late," he assured. "I'm going to stop at my house and look for food, so I'll be a little longer."

"Take good care," the group called as he walked out. Ulmer sat silently in a corner.

As the evening grew late, the residents of the cellar began puzzling as to when Ingelfinger would come. Finally they concluded that he had been detained and decided to spend the night in his own house. They all went to sleep anticipating his return.

As the group began to stir the next morning, footsteps on the floor above them sent a wave of excitement through the cellar. Frau Ingelfinger rushed toward the steps to greet her husband.

"Irene!" she gasped. "I thought you were my husband." She backed into the room, as her young neighbor walked in with a solemn expression. Her voice quivering, the older woman asked, "Is—there something wrong?"

"Please sit down, Frau," the woman said softly. Frau Ingelfinger sat on a bench, trembling. "Herr Ingelfinger died early this morning at the Children's Clinic. He was wounded by an explosion."

The widow slumped, face in her hands, and wailed loudly; several people gathered around trying to console her. Kurt turned and stared at Ulmer who's turn it had been for that trip. Ulmer fidgeted and stared at the wall.

As he had passed the Staufenbergschule, Ingelfinger was struck in the leg by an exploding shell. Helpless, he lay in the street and cried out. No one was nearby. Late in the night, he was discovered, barely conscious, by passersby. He was rushed to the Children's Clinic in Sontheim, but he had lost too much blood. In a few hours he was dead.

Despite the mourning, there was no time to despair. The food supply was low and the water was gone. The chicken soup had sufficed for the evening's meal, but there was little left. Kurt, realizing the immediacy of the problem, snatched up a bucket with his good arm and announced, "Look for me in about an hour. I'll go to the Bord bakery first, and then to the Deinenbach for water." He ran up the steps.

Outside, he heard an airplane and looked up. It was a spotter plane; if he was noticed, the observers might direct artillery fire or fighters to strafe the area. Desperately he lunged toward a nearby tree and waited for the plane to fly out of sight. As soon as it seemed safe, he dashed down the street toward the bakery. Several times shells hit nearby, but he kept going. Breathless, he ran into the bakery.

"Herr Bord," he gasped, "Herr Ingelfinger was killed on the way here yesterday, so we didn't get any bread. Can you give us two today?"

The baker shook his head. "Sorry, but I had no bread left from yesterday. I can only sell you one loaf."

Kurt grimaced. "But we are 26 people!"

"I wish I could give you more," the man said with a shrug. "Come back tomorrow; maybe I can do something for you then."

With a sigh, Kurt put the loaf into the pail, laid his money on the counter and dashed out of the store. As he ran toward the Deinenbach, shells were hitting frequently. Sprinting down the street, he murmured, "Lord, help me to get back safely! The people need this bread." At the creek, he took the bread and stuffed it inside his sling. After filling the bucket, he trotted across the field as fast as he could without spilling the water.

As he neared the Lenzes' house, the bucket seemed unbearably heavy. For a moment Kurt set it down and flexed his arm. Close behind him a shell exploded. He swung his arm down to retrieve the bucket and bolted toward the house.

When he entered the basement, the group greeted him excitedly. Kurt set the bucket on a small table and stopped to catch his breath. Finally he pulled out the solitary loaf. "I'm sorry, but this was all Herr Bord could spare us." There was a chorus of groans. Kurt tried to sound as cheerful as possible. "I may be able to get more tomorrow; we'll just have to do with less today. Let's be thankful for the food that we still have."

"But the children are crying, and we are all hungry," a woman moaned.

Kurt nodded seriously. "I know. My stomach is growling, too." He thought for a few seconds, then beamed. "We will pray!" he exclaimed. The people stared cynically. "Come. Everybody kneel where you are, and I will ask the Lord to help us. He gave the Israelites food in the wilderness, so why can't He give us bread? And if He doesn't give us food, He will certainly help us to get by without!" The people relented and knelt on the floor while Kurt prayed. A sense of peace and contentment seemed to enter the crowded cellar.

The next day, Kurt ventured to the baker again. Herr Bord seemed much friendlier that afternoon. The group in the cellar was elated when Kurt returned with two loaves of bread. It was now Saturday, April 7, Kurt and Ruth's third night in Lenzes' cellar. Outside, the explosions increased in frequency. Even the unbelieving in the cellar began to whisper prayers for protection.

As the American guns pounded Heilbronn and its suburbs, the Wehrmacht prepared itself for retreat. Saturday night, the soldiers blew up the footbridge over the Neckar connecting Sontheim and Böckingen. The following night, the people in the cellar were suddenly wakened as the earth shivered with the impact of a huge explosion. The Wehrmacht had just destroyed eight train cars filled with German ammunition.

The next morning Kurt walked to his home to check for damage. The streets were strewn with plaster, roofing tiles, glass and telephone cables. Few houses had been spared by the blast. Not a window was left in the Ziefles' house. The roof had been jarred loose, and the stone wall in front of the house had shifted. But the damage was minimal compared to some of the other houses closer to the explosion.

The battle grew in intensity in the following days. The

fight for Heilbronn became so violent that it was later referred to as "Little Stalingrad." Mortars, shells, and grenades pummelled the streets and houses incessantly. Night after night fires broke out, but all major fire-fighting equipment had already been removed from the area. It seemed evident that the Nazi forces could not hold out for long.

As Kurt ran toward the bakery on the following Wednesday, he came upon a pile of German army rifles alongside Staufenbergstrasse; a strange sense of elation rose inside of him. "The Americans are here—it's all over," he said aloud.

During the night American troops using boats, crossed the Neckar River two miles southwest of Sontheim. On the north, Heilbronn's defenses crumbled.

The group sat helplessly in the cellar, listening to the sounds of combat—the crack and thump of rifles and grenades, and the clanking growl of tanks. As Thursday wore on, it was obvious that Sontheim had been overrun by the Americans. During the night, the shooting stopped.

The residents of the cellar slept little. The morning held only foreboding mystery. Kurt and Ruth did their best to calm the people, but faith came hard for those who had entrusted their future to the Thousand-Year Reich.

About nine o'clock in the morning, two green-clad American soldiers cautiously entered the cellar. Fortunately, Kurt had not worn his Air Force uniform since his accident. Satisfied that no German soldiers were in the house, the Americans departed. To the amazement of the occupants, the soldiers had been very friendly. The attitude of such gracious conquerors quelled much of their fear. There would be curfews and restrictions, and shortages would still persist; but now they could return to their homes in safety.

In Maubach, things were still the same. Sometimes enemy planes flew over, but they were always heading somewhere else. Cannons and bombs were only read about. Only when the body of a fallen son arrived did war again become a harsh reality.

Maria and Helmut slowly walked around the little farming neighborhood as the sun was disappearing. Her phlebitis made walking painful, but Maria needed the time to think. Helmut skipped and ran about, chasing bugs and discovering the spring flowers. She smiled at his antics.

"Mama! May I save these and give them to Ruth?" he asked, holding up a brightly-colored bunch.

She had not heard anything from Ruth and Kurt since she had left Sontheim a week-and-a-half before, and now even her staunch faith seemed battered and wobbly. But she dared not unveil her fears to her little one. She bit her lip and nodded to him.

Helmut suddenly halted his antics, seeming to sense his mother's seriousness. "I wish Papa were here," he said. "Will he come soon?"

Maria groped for confidence. "I'm sure he will come home soon, Helmut, don't worry." *God, don't let me lie to my son.*

X
Saturday, April 14, 1945

*And shall not God avenge his own elect, which cry
day and night unto him, though he bear long with
them? I tell you that he will avenge them speedily.*

—Luke 18:7, 8

"Herr and Frau Schiele! When did you arrive here in
Maubach?" Maria had last seen the couple in Sontheim
where they had taken refuge in a home near the Ziefles'
after fleeing from the Red Army advance on Eastern Germany. To Maria's surprise, they now were walking past the
Haiers' house in Maubach.

"We are just passing through on our way south," replied
Herr Schiele tiredly. "We never expected to be on the road
so soon again, but the Americans are closing in."

Maria leaped at the chance to find out about her family.
"Have you seen or heard from my children, Kurt and
Ruth?" She asked anxiously. "They stayed behind when I
came here."

Schiele hesitated before answering. "I haven't been in
contact with them, but . . . everything near the Ackermann
factory was destroyed when the Wehrmacht blew up some
ammunition cars. I'm very sorry."

Maria cupped her hand over her mouth and trembled.
"Are—are you sure?"

"I saw the wreckage myself."

Maria turned her head away as her composure dissolved. She suddenly felt weak. "Excuse me, I must go inside," she murmured, and hurried toward the door. The Schieles walked on.

Feeling faint, Maria slumped into a chair. Seeing the distress in his mother's face, Helmut ran to her and laid his head on her lap, hugging her legs. Mutely she patted his shoulder, hanging onto her composure for his sake. Fortunately, Helmut's bedtime was near.

Solitude became oppressive as her fears closed in on her. She could not face alone the possibility of such a tragedy. Shoulders heaving with suppressed emotion, she rushed to Berta who was sewing in the living room and collapsed on her shoulder. Between sobs, Maria disclosed the news the Schieles had given. Berta sat helpless and silent. She had always looked to her oldest sister for counsel; it seemed impossible that Maria was now looking to her. All she could do was help Maria to her bedroom and trust that the following day would bring better tidings.

Maria lay on her bed and buried her face in the pillow to muffle her sobs from sleeping Helmut. *God, have you betrayed me? Has my family finally been destroyed? It seems impossible, but I don't want to hide from the truth. Please, somehow show me if they are dead or alive.*

The next morning was Sunday. Maria sat silently at her breakfast. If she only could know for sure, it would somewhat ease the terrible burden. There was something horribly cruel in having to *assume* your children were dead. The complete truth, even though tragic, would have been so much less painful and frustrating than presumption.

The family finished eating and began to clean up. Christian left to search for Stefan, his Polish laborer, a war prisoner who had not reported for work in two days. Only a few minutes later there was a loud knocking at the door. Helmut ran downstairs and opened it. He found himself peering up at a tall Prussian army captain.

"Show me your identity cards," he demanded gruffly as Maria and Berta appeared. The women anxiously hurried to their rooms, then returned with their documents.

The officer examined the documents. Without looking up, he grunted, "Aha! Frau Ziefle, you are not from Maubach. Correct?"

Puzzled, she replied, "That is right."

"I have orders to draft all dispensable individuals immediately, to defend the fatherland. Since you are only a guest in this house, you must come with me. We will teach you how to use a gun."

"Sir! I have a six-year-old son who needs his mother!"

The officer glared at her. "For the fatherland, no sacrifice is too great! If you do not come immediately, I will have you executed as a traitor!"

Maria glanced at Helmut. He stood frozen with fear, obviously understanding to some degree what was happening. Suddenly he began to cry loudly.

"Shut up, boy!" the man snapped. But Helmut persisted.

Berta could not restrain herself any longer. "Sir, I need my sister—there is too much work in this household for me to do alone. Besides, she has phlebitis—she could not take the strain of combat."

"Every second that the enemy is delayed helps our defenses!" The soldier was furious. "A life means nothing if it cannot be sacrificed for Deutschland!"

"Please, sir! I beg you to leave my sister here! I need her!"

The man gave Berta a strange stare. Without another word he angrily stamped past the women and began searching through the house for deserters. In a few moments he stalked out, slamming the door behind him. He would search every house in Maubach before he was satisfied.

Maria and Berta stared at each other, puzzled. "I don't know why he changed his mind so suddenly," Maria said with a faint smile, "but I know it was a miracle! It was almost as if he saw or heard someone in this room whom we weren't aware of." She patted Helmut who had attached himself tightly to her legs. "Thank the Lord we can still be together!"

Berta turned and headed toward the stairs. "We had better get busy baking some more zwieback, eh? We never know when we'll have to start using it." Maria and Helmut followed.

For several days the people of Maubach had known that the Americans would come soon. Everyone was nervously making preparations. Berta and Maria had busied themselves by baking large quantities of the hard toast and storing it in the cellar in case of a siege or food shortage. They also had plenty of canned meat and sausage. The days ahead were uncertain, but a good stock of food was reassuring. And the activity kept Maria from succumbing to her nagging fears about her family.

Each day, tension in the village increased. Rumors flourished in the uncertainty, and Maria and Berta tried hard not to believe horror stories they heard concerning the advancing American armies. On Thursday morning, the Prussian captain with a handful of his conscripts hastened out of Maubach on a horse-drawn cart. The people supposed that the end was now imminent.

Early that afternoon, Stefan, Christian's farm laborer, returned—but not alone. With him were twenty other Poles who had been captive workers at nearby farms and businesses. With a strange arrogance, they took over Christian's shop and the food cellar. Casting civility aside, they talked and sang raucously, brandishing sharp knives. When the Nazis had invaded Poland, these people had been shipped to Germany as human plunder. For five years they had been virtually slaves. The roles were now being reversed. With the American armies approaching, the Poles flaunted their inevitable freedom, and their German masters were powerless to control their prisoners. Many Eastern laborers would seek revenge against their overseers. Fortunately for Christian and Berta, they had been kind to Stefan.

The women did not dare to enter the cellar any longer.

"There goes all our meat and zwieback," Berta sighed. "All we have left is this one tin of bread in the kitchen."

Maria was staring out the window. "All the farmers are coming back from the fields already," she observed. "Look, Berta! Some of the neighbors are hanging sheets and pillowcases out their windows for white flags! The Americans must be coming!"

Berta paled. "Maria, what will we do? What will they do to us?"

Maria sensed a fresh surge of confidence in her spirit as she approached her sister and put her arm around her. "The Lord knows what will happen. Let's trust Him to pull us through." Berta nodded nervously.

"Let's go outside and find out what is happening," Maria suggested. She turned toward the adjoining room and called, "Helmut! Let's go outside!" Her son scurried through the door and down the stairs ahead of the women. Christian already had been outside visiting with a neighbor, and he hurried to join them when he saw them step out into the street.

In the street, several people, their faces tense, conversed in small groups. A strange noise caught Maria's attention; in the distance was a muffled, droning growl. She thought back to the dreadful night in December, but this was different—it was not the sound of airplanes.

"We'd better go back into the house," Christian suggested. "We'll probably be safer there." The women and Helmut followed him upstairs. From the living room they could observe the event from an open window. The whole village watched as if a parade were approaching.

In minutes, a long line of dark green trucks, jeeps and tanks moved through the streets of Maubach. The citizens watched spellbound.

"Mama!" Helmut exclaimed, "there's a man with black skin in that tank!"

"They are called Negroes, Helmut. Many of them live in America." Helmut continued to stare in fascination.

A captain walked toward the house, looking up at the window. "Are you Polish?" he shouted in English. The four at the window looked at each other and shrugged their shoulders.

"Are you Polish?" he shouted louder.

"I think he's asking if we're Poles," Christian suggested. He and Berta and Maria shook their heads at the officer.

"Raus! Raus!" he yelled back. "You have twenty minutes to get out."

The party in the window again shrugged their shoulders and shook their heads; none of them understood the English part of the command. The captain, with improvised sign language, finally made them understand. Quickly the four grabbed the zwieback from the kitchen, two blankets from a bedroom, then hurried down to the street. They were now refugees.

The family walked along the street toward the public bakehouse, the nearest building. Inside, they found the fire in the oven still burning. "My, isn't this cozy," Christian joked. "Maybe there's some bread in here as well." He looked in the oven; two large, fragrant loaves of farmer's bread were baking. He pulled them out and said, "These should take care of us for at least four days!"

As he spoke, a neighbor girl walked in and picked up her two loaves. Disappointed, Christian dropped down on a bench.

A black soldier wearily tramped into the room. "Raus! Raus!"

"Not again!" Christian shook his head impatiently.

The soldier did his best to explain that the German forces who had retreated hastily were planning a counter-attack for the evening; the bakehouse would be in the line of fire. Somehow the little group got the message and left. Now they would have to find another place to stay.

"Sorry, our cellar is full." They would try the next house.

"Four people? We don't have that much room left." They trudged on.

"Try Grubers next door, they might be able to help." It was shattering to be turned away by one's own neighbors. The sun was setting.

Desperate, they tried the farmer Sachs. "Frau Sachs," Christian began, "the Americans have forced us out of our house. Could we stay with you?"

"I wish I could help you, Herr Haier, but we already have too many staying in our cellar."

"We can't sleep on the grass tonight!" Christian was disgusted. "How about if we sleep upstairs?"

The woman looked at him astonished. "You want to stay up here when the shooting starts?" She flapped her arm at him. "It's all yours, if you're crazy enough to try it. But we're spending the night in the cellar."

Christian turned to the women and asked in weary desperation, "Well, what should we do?"

Berta answered instantly, "We'll take it—won't we, Maria?"

"We don't have much choice," Maria conceded.

Upstairs, they found two beautiful bedrooms. The eiderdown quilts and clean white bedsheets were much more inviting than a damp, crowded cellar.

"Mama, will we be killed when the battle starts?" Helmut asked innocently.

"No, I don't think so," Maria answered. "The Lord has protected us through this war, and I trust He'll continue to. Let's get you ready for bed." As she undressed him, she called Christian and Berta to join them for a time of prayer.

The four sat on Helmut's bed together. "We must pray for the Lord's protection tonight." They all bowed their heads, and each prayed in turn, remembering the family members who were not with them.

As Christian and Berta left for their bedroom, Maria tucked Helmut in. "Sleep well," she said. "God is with us." She kissed him and turned away, her heart crying out, *Lord, this could be a terrible night. If Helmut wakes up, he will be horribly frightened by all the noise. Please, please keep him asleep all night.* She climbed into her bed.

Within the hour, German artillery unleashed its fury against the American forces in the village. The American gunners immediately returned the fire, filling the air with the screams and blasts of explosive shells. Berta and Maria rose from their beds and joined each other in the hallway to pray. Their vigil lasted the whole night. Maria prayed much for her little son.

Christian came into the hall, angrily muttering, "This is insane! Our armies are beaten, so why don't they surrender instead of shooting on their own people?" The women agreed. But the firing did not cease until the sun was ready to rise.

As sunlight began to gleam through the window, Helmut stirred and opened his eyes. He turned and saw his mother sleeping on the other bed. The air was quiet. "We're alive!" he called. "Mama, the Lord kept us alive!"

Maria turned wearily toward her son and smiled in spite of her tiredness. "And he kept you asleep, Helmut. The noise of the guns was terrible, but you never woke up!" She pulled her covers closer. "Play quietly for a little while so that Mama can get some sleep."

Later Berta came in and awakened her sister. With Christian, they proceeded downstairs. The Sachs and some of their companions were in the kitchen eating.

"We want to thank you for the use of your house last night," said Christian to the Sachs.

"It was nothing," Frau Sachs replied. "Here, sit down and eat. The least I can do is feed you." Gratefully the four accepted her invitation.

One of the men spoke. "You are either brave or stupid—we never expected to see you folks alive this morning!"

"It was the Lord who kept us," Maria said seriously. "We spent most of the night praying. I'm glad it's over!"

Berta interrupted. "You'll be very crowded in here now, so I suppose we'll have to find another place to stay."

Frau Sachs replied, "I wish we had room for you. Why

don't you try the Schultzes down the street?"

As soon as they finished their meal, they thanked their hosts again, then walked out into the street. The town crier was coming toward them. They stopped to listen for his announcement: the Americans had instituted a 22-hour curfew, from 11:00 a.m. to 9:00 a.m. Fortunately, it was just 9 o'clock, so they had the full two hours to find new lodging.

Tired of this endless search, Christian suggested, "Berta, why don't we check our house? Maybe we could return there."

"I'd rather stay there than in someone else's home," she agreed.

When they reached their house, however, they discovered that the Americans had moved in and set up temporary quarters. Disappointed, they retraced their steps and approached the Schultz family.

Herr and Frau Schultz, an elderly couple, were happy to accommodate the four wanderers. They also had gleaned information about the aftermath of the last night's fighting; a large number of livestock had been killed and some buildings were destroyed; most saddening were the civilian casualties—several were wounded, and a ten-year-old girl was killed. Maria sensed afresh the pain of not knowing the fate of Kurt, Ruth, and her husband.

Confined by the curfew, the Ziefles and Haiers spent the remainder of the day keeping themselves occupied. The women helped Frau Schultz cook and sew. Christian discussed farming and the war with Herr Schultz for a while, then found a book that intrigued him. Helmut played with the cat.

During the two hours of freedom that day, rumors had multiplied among the residents of Maubach. Especially frightening to Helmut was the claim that if Americans caught children breaking curfew, they would haul them away in trucks, never to be seen again. But young minds forget easily.

The next morning, about 8:30, Helmut stepped out the

back door to play in the small yard. Just across the fence, an American soldier patrolled the street, enforcing the curfew; his head toward Helmut. Helmut dashed into the house and hid behind the door in terror. Nothing happened. Still frightened, though, he spent the rest of the morning close to his mother.

As soon as the curfew had lifted, Berta, Maria, and Helmut walked back to the Haiers' house to find more blankets—the Schultzes' house had been rather cold at night. Maria had brought her best blankets from Heilbronn to Christian and Berta's. Helmut dreaded meeting more soldiers on the street; he was glad to be with his mother.

A corporal with a rifle hanging from his shoulder barred entrance to the house. Helmut timidly clutched his mother's dress. "Sir, this is my sister's house," Maria said slowly, hoping the man would understand. "We would like to go in and get some blankets we left behind—we were forced to leave on sudden notice."

The guard stared blankly. "Captain," he finally answered.

Not sure what he meant, the trio stepped toward the door. The soldier maneuvered to stay in front of them. "Captain," he said again, but they kept moving closer. He raised his voice. "Captain! Captain! Captain!" But the language barrier was too great. Frantically he pulled the rifle from his shoulder and pointed it toward them.

"Mama! Please, don't go any farther!" Helmut cried out, pulling at his mother's arm. She stopped.

"Captain!" the man said loudly, pointing his finger toward a building down the street. Finally they understood and went to find his superior. Fortunately, the captain could speak some German, and he gave permission to enter the house.

Maria went in alone. When she reached the top of the stairs and entered the living quarters, she gasped in horror. Drawers and closets had been emptied, and the contents were littered all over the floor. Five large, unshaven soldiers were sprawled on the two sofas and armchairs. She sensed their discomfiting stares. Maria quickly moved to the hutch, pulled out the four blankets, and hurried down the steps, retreating from the unnerving eyes.

There was still an hour left before curfew, so the three decided to check the Haiers' garden plot just outside the village. As they walked toward the garden, they came to a spot which afforded a clear view of the highway. They were overwhelmed by the sight. A seemingly endless column of trucks and jeeps rumbled toward Stuttgart; they had never seen so much military equipment.

"Mama, may I stay here and watch the cars and trucks while you look at the garden?" Helmut begged.

Maria and Berta glanced at each other hesitantly. "If you promise to stay right here and not move," Maria finally agreed. Helmut nodded eagerly.

The two women went on to the garden. To their relief, they found it had been unharmed by the shelling two nights earlier. They spent some time pulling weeds and enjoying the fresh air. Soon the curfew was almost upon them, and they hurried to retrieve Helmut and go home.

When they reached Helmut, the line of vehicles was still passing, with no sign of its ending. Maria wondered at the sight: *what kind of nation is this, that has so much military might?* It seemed ridiculous that Germany had even attempted to fight such an army.

Briskly they walked home, not wanting to be caught on the streets after 11:00. At home they were greeted by Christian with the good news that the curfew had been lifted, except for night hours. He had also heard that in about a week the Americans would vacate houses which they had commandeered.

Maria's heart leaped at the news. Could it be that the war was almost over? It was as if her soul had been released after six years of imprisonment. The godless Reich had been crushed. She wept silently. She did not know where her husband was, her eldest was at the Russian Front, and her second son and only daughter were possibly dead; yet she was finally free. No more "Heil Hitler," no more persecution of innocent people, no more bombings. Germany was again at peace.

The soldiers that spoke the strange language were not overly friendly to the Germans yet. After a long bloody war, they could not help but be suspicious of the people who were seemingly responsible for oppressing and killing millions.

But Helmut was fascinated by the invaders. Most enticing to him was the food these soldiers ate. He had experienced hunger for as long as he could remember, and here were people who had all they could eat and more. Deliberately he would stand close to the cooks' tent, hoping for a handout. His eyes nearly popped out when he saw scrambled eggs filling a pan so big he could have lain down in it; and he had never seen so much bread as the day two trucks, bulging with loaves, pulled up to be unloaded.

But all this abundance was denied the local citizens. Painfully they endured the humiliation of defeat and their loss of rights.

Finally the Haiers and Ziefles were allowed to move back to their house. Maria had warned Christian and Berta about the mess she had seen inside; but after a week, it was even worse. Berta cried out with horror at the sight. Clothing, books, utensils and important papers were strewn everywhere. A quick check revealed that the soldiers had only taken items they considered souvenirs of the Nazi era. The family set about to restore order.

Maria had become increasingly concerned to find out the truth about Kurt and Ruth, and she wanted to return to Sontheim and discover it for herself. But she had no idea how to make the trip. The open countryside was still not completely secured by the Americans; also, many resentful Eastern Europeans who had been POW's were staying out in the country, making travel risky.

Finally she approached the American captain and asked his advice. He suggested she go to the nearby village of Backnang and secure permission from his commander to go to Sontheim.

The biggest obstacle in the trek to Backnang turned out to be Helmut. They both were fearful as they left the relative safety of Maubach. When they walked past the last houses of Maubach and faced the open fields, Helmut panicked and began to cry. "I won't go," he insisted as tears rained down his cheeks.

"Don't be scared, Helmut," Maria assured, "I'm going with you."

"No, we'll be shot! I just know we will."

Maria tried to pull him along, but he resisted, stamping his feet and crying even louder. She had never seen her son so stubborn. Finally she picked him up and soundly spanked him. Whimpering, he followed grudgingly.

The trip was a waste of time. The commander refused to allow a woman and child to travel alone. Crushed, Maria and Helmut trudged homeward. She was glad Helmut was too busy observing her surroundings to notice her tears. Silently she pleaded, *What am I to do, Lord? I need to know the truth about my children. Please make a way for me.* Discouragement drained her last reserves of strength as she walked.

Finally they reached Maubach and turned down the street to the Haier home. A shout caught her attention— "Mama! Mama!" She eyed the house. Someone was waving an arm wildly from a second-story window. Then she saw the other arm hanging still—in a large white cast.

"It's Kurt!" Helmut yelled, and dashed ahead of his mother.

Fresh energy surged through her and she quickened her pace. "Thank you, Lord, for answering my prayers!" Maria said aloud as she neared the door. She hurried up the stairs and tearfully gathered Kurt in her arms. "God is so good!" she cried out.

She stepped back and looked him over. "What about Ruth?"

"Oh, she's fine. She can't wait to see you!"

"You don't know how much this means, Kurt! I've just tried to secure permission for traveling to Sontheim, but the commander denied it because it was too risky. I had to find out the truth, because some people from Sontheim told me that everything near the Ackermann factory was destroyed—and that you were probably dead." She hugged him again. "I can hardly believe this is happening!"

"Those people were mistaken," Kurt assured her. "Our house is still standing, though the roof was knocked loose by an explosion. But I've already fixed it. And the factory was only partially damaged."

"Have you heard anything from Papa?" Maria asked eagerly.

Kurt's expression became serious. "No. And Berta told me you don't know about him either. We'll have to keep praying for him as well as for Reinhold."

"Mama, how about leaving for home tomorrow morning? Ruth is expecting us."

"The sooner the better," Maria replied. "But how did you come here? By bicycle?"

"It wasn't easy with my cast, but I rode all the way."

Berta and Christian preferred that the Ziefles would wait until the countryside was safer, but they understood their longing to be reunited in their own house. In the morning Berta fed them a hearty breakfast and supplied them with boiled eggs and sandwiches to eat on the way. After a short time of prayer together, the three set out on their 30-mile trip.

Kurt's bicycle was so loaded with luggage that no one could ride it. It was difficult to push it with only one arm, but he valiantly took over his task, Maria helping to steady the bike. Thankfully, the weather was beautiful.

The route, though flanked by spring's bright fresh colors, was marred by the remnants of war. There were countless anti-tank obstacles; the roads were pocked with shell-craters; blown-up bridges lay twisted in the streams; many fields bore scars from the ravages of artillery; abandoned German tanks, trucks, and mobile artillery stood in ghostly silence.

Helmut bravely kept up with the two adults; they walked as fast as possible to reach home before the evening. Every few miles they would stop and rest, but only for a few minutes. At Grossbottwar, twelve miles from Sontheim, extremely thirsty, they searched until they found a farmer who would give them milk. Refreshed, they went on.

About four miles from home, Helmut pleaded, "Can't we sit down? I'm too tired to walk anymore." They stopped and let him rest.

Kurt grinned at his brother. "A soldier in Sontheim gave me a chocolate bar, Helmut. If you'll be brave and walk all the way home, I'll give it to you!"

Helmut leaped to his feet, exclaiming, "Chocolate!" He puffed out his little chest and set his face resolutely. "I'm going to make it anyway, chocolate or no chocolate!"

"That's the spirit!" Kurt replied, tousling Helmut's hair.

It was after four o'clock as they approached Sontheim. When they were less than a quarter-mile from the first house, the rhythm of their footsteps was suddenly interrupted by the "thwang!" of rifle bullets hitting the field next to them. Kurt dropped the bike and pulled Helmut and Maria to the ground.

"This is ridiculous!" he muttered. "We come all this way without trouble, then die in sight of our town!" He looked around. "The shots must be coming from those trees over there; I wonder who it is? Maybe some angry Poles."

The shooting subsided; after waiting a while, the three Ziefles slowly stood up and brushed themselves off. Kurt picked up the bike and started moving. "Let's go as fast as we can!" he ordered. "They might start shooting again." Summoning all their energy, they hurried toward the town, all three pushing the bicycle together. As they reached the shelter of the houses, they slowed their pace, their hearts pounding and lungs aching.

Finally at their own house, Maria and Helmut rushed up the stairs to see Ruth. "We're home, Ruth!" Helmut shrieked, running ahead of his mother. And there she stood at the head of the stairs, smiling and holding out her arms. The three eagerly embraced.

Ruth had already cooked supper for them, but Maria first collapsed on the sofa and rested her aching legs and feet. Though she had not complained, the last half of the trip had been agony for her. Kurt and Helmut joined her. Their furniture had never felt so good. It had been more than three weeks since Maria and Helmut had left.

"Well, before we eat, we must thank God for reuniting us," Maria announced. The others knelt with her beside the sofa. "And we must pray especially for Papa and Reinhold."

As they finished praying, a clattering noise on the street caught their attention. Kurt went to the window and looked. "There's a strange man coming up to our house."

The others joined him at the window. A man pushing a rickety baby carriage was approaching their door. He was unshaven, and on his ragged jacket was a large white "P."

"He must be a Pole," Maria said quietly. "I'll go see what he wants." She went downstairs and opened the door.

Their eyes met, and the two people stood speechless for a moment. "George!" Maria cried as they hugged each other. "We didn't know if you were dead or alive!"

George straightened up and grinned at his wife. "It's obvious I'm not dead!" The children dashed down the stairs to greet their father; gleefully they gathered around him.

As they ushered him upstairs to the dining room, he began telling his story. "I dumped the files I was hauling in Lake Constance. Then my unit went to Sigmaringen to stay until we received further orders. However, the Americans arrived in less than a week. We were all arrested, of course, but they released me after three days when they confirmed that I wasn't a Nazi. Oh—I almost forgot!" He reached into his pocket and pulled out a chocolate bar. "An American soldier gave this to me. I want you to have it, Helmut."

Helmut's eyes grew big. "Two chocolate bars in one day! This is better than a birthday!"

George continued. "I walked to Maubach to find you, and arrived two hours after you left. I had brought the baby carriage in case Helmut became tired of walking. Anyway, Berta told me about your stay with her and about Kurt coming to bring you home. As soon as she had fed me, I came to Sontheim as fast as I could."

"But why are you wearing that awful jacket? Isn't it for Polish prisoners?" Kurt asked.

George laughed. "With the Americans imprisoning Nazis, and many Poles acting like bandits, it's a lot safer right now to travel as a Pole."

"I'm just glad we're all safe," Maria concluded. "Tonight we can all go to bed early and get some rest. This house is going to need much fixing tomorrow." Maria's eyes welled up. "My only wish is that Reinhold were here with us."

May 1945

And the Lord shall help them, and deliver them: he shall deliver them from the wicked, and save them, because they trust in him.

—Psalm 37:40

George Ziefle walked slowly through the gate and into his yard, his shoulders drooping. He halted and looked nervously around at his family. Maria and Ruth were hanging laundry; Kurt and Helmut were chopping wood for the stove. Ruth turned her head and saw her father. "Any letters, Papa?" she inquired eagerly.

George walked closer and his hands trembled as he drew an envelope from his shirt pocket. "Come here—all of you." His voice was strained. The others soberly gathered around him as he took a sheet of paper from the envelope and held it before them. "This is from the government. Reinhold was captured by the Russian army last month and is a prisoner of war."

Maria gasped, her hand over her mouth. She snatched the letter from her husband's hand to read it for herself.

George stared woodenly ahead as he explained, "According to the letter, he was captured in the Spreeforest while retreating after the fall of Berlin." He hesitated, and his voice dropped. "I am afraid for his safety—I've been told the Russians can be very cruel. We must face the fact that we may never see him again."

"No," Maria said firmly, though her face was already streaked with tears. "He will not die. I cannot believe that the Lord has brought our family safely this far only to allow Reinhold to die. These are hard days, but we will be together again—I am sure."

Kurt spoke solemnly. "I don't have as much faith as Mama, but I think she is right. I think if we pray, God will keep our brother." Then with a wry grin, "Maybe an angel will take him out, just like Saint Peter in the Bible!" Their faces softened at his remark.

"Mama, you pray right now," George suggested. She nodded and the others bowed their heads.

Maria's voice trembled as she began. "I thank you, God, that you know our sorrows. You have watched over us through this war and have kept us all alive—thank you for miracles. But now again we are helpless! Please take good care of Reinhold, wherever he is—we want to have him with us again. Cause his captors to be merciful." Her voice caught.

"We also know, Lord, that you did not keep your Son from death. So we say, as Jesus said before He was arrested, 'Not my will, but Thine be done.' Amen."

The family chorused in low voices, "Amen."

"I will go make some lunch," Maria announced matter-of-factly. The rest returned to their work until she called.

Making lunch was more easily said than done. Those first weeks after the war had been brutally harsh. All utilities were still inoperative. Water had to be carried from the Deinenbach; light came only from the wood stove and from the one skinny candle rationed to them each week at the city hall.

Food was the main struggle. The family was allowed one loaf of bread each week, in addition to what little else might be available. The Ziefles took turns standing in long lines to receive bread, a small measure of oatmeal, or a quart of watery, bluish milk.

In marked contrast, the American forces who had set up headquarters in the Ackermann facilities only a block from the Ziefle home enjoyed a variety and abundance of food and traveled freely.

Fortunately, it was springtime, and the Ziefles would soon have food from their garden. Their dozen hens supplemented their diet with eggs.

None of the family was able to find employment yet, so each member was busy with the task of survival. Working in the garden, chopping firewood, and collecting grass and other food for the chickens not only provided necessary food and heat but also kept each person occupied both physically and mentally.

Food shortages and other hardships, though, were mere inconveniences to the Ziefles and other Germans compared to the lawlessness of the vengeful Poles and other Eastern Europeans who now roamed through the city and countryside. The Allies had provided food and housing for many of them at the old military barracks in Heilbronn; but now free from German oppression, they wanted no restrictions. Unlike the German citizenry, the East Europeans were not under travel restrictions. And since they were not under close scrutiny, many of them carried weapons.

Some of these foreigners broke into homes in broad daylight, robbing and terrorizing the German families. They would butcher livestock at will, gorging themselves on the meat. A German attempting to stop them was taking his life in his hands. One local farmer tried to prevent two Poles from picking his cherries and was brutally murdered with his own sickle.

George straightened up and happily looked at the season's first three gladiolas he had just picked; Maria would be delighted. Soon the dozens of green stalks around him would be exploding with color.

"How much for those flowers?" said a voice gruffly. George turned to see two Poles approaching him from behind.

He did not want to part with them, so he suggested an absurd price: "Three Marks."

One of the men reached into his jacket pocket and pulled out a knife, deftly flicking it open. He pointed the blade at George's stomach and glared icily. "Give them to me."

George glanced down at the menacing blade. He had heard enough reports to know that these men would not hesitate to kill him, even for three flowers. His heart pounding, he quickly handed them to the man. The pair turned toward each other and laughed, then sauntered away.

Dejected, George went home and told Maria about the incident. She was horrified at the thought of losing her husband over flowers. *We thought the danger was over when the war was finished, Lord. Now we live in danger of being murdered by these lawless thugs. Change their hearts, and protect us.*

A political struggle for survival also began among the formerly adamant Nazis. As soon as Germany had surrendered, those who had harassed and sometimes brutalized the Germans who refused to cooperate with the Nazi cause became strangely docile and benevolent. The Ziefles found it strange to see people who shortly before had scoffed at religious faith suddenly sitting in the front pews of the church, attentively absorbing Pastor Brendle's sermons. Fearing that the victims of their persecution would lodge complaints and have them arrested, they hoped their new-found piety would move the courts to be lenient toward them. The Ziefles were also baffled when neighbors who treated them so coldly during the war now greeted them with dramatic warmth. Maria could not help feeling a sense of justice as she saw some of these people taken away for questioning by the new authorities.

Just as remarkable was the about-face in the editorial viewpoint of the local newspaper, the *Heilbronner Stimme*. Preceding the fall of the Third Reich, the paper pleaded for the citizens to give a superhuman effort in defense of the

Fatherland. The Führer's words had been quoted as if they were divine proclamations.

In the first issue after the surrender, the *Stimme* bore the headline, "No More War for 99 Years." The editorial which followed suggested that Germany ban and never again manufacture any type of weapon—including knives. This sharp attack on war and weaponry and the strong support for a peaceful society almost had biblical overtones.

I am puzzled—perplexed at this sudden blossoming of civility. How can men be hateful and barbaric, then suddenly become virtuous and gentle? I know, Lord that you can change hearts—you did it for Kurt—but I do not hear any talk of God from these people. I wish that what I have seen on the outside would reflect a change on the inside; show them that their own righteousness is only filthy rags without the real change that only God's Spirit can bring.

Each day one of the Ziefles hurried to the post office, longing to receive some news from Reinhold. When mail delivery was finally restored, the family eagerly waited each day for the postman to come through their neighborhood. They still did not know even where he was interned; any mail they sent was routed through a central Russian military address. They had sent Reinhold two packages of food they were able to spare.

One morning late in the summer, Kurt and Helmut were playing ball in the yard when they saw the postman approaching. "I'll race you!" Helmut challenged his brother as he began running toward the man. Kurt purposely allowed his little brother to take the lead and receive the delivery. Helmut, puffing, turned toward Kurt with a letter clutched in his hand. "Look, Kurt!" He turned the envelope toward him so he could read it. "Where is it from?"

Kurt studied the stampings on the paper. "It's from eastern Germany. I'll bet it's from Reinhold! Let's take it up to Mama and Papa." The two scrambled into the house and up the stairs.

With trembling fingers, George Ziefle ripped open the envelope. Nervously he pulled out the thin gray paper, then glanced at the signature. "This is from Reinhold!"

Most of the letter had been defaced with heavy black marks—censoring by prison officials. All that was left was the assurance that Reinhold was in good health and that he was temporarily in eastern Germany. He also noted that only one prisoner, someone named Ochs from Karlsruhe, a town near Heilbronn, had received any packages.

"That means that the two packages we sent never reached him," said Kurt sadly. "I wish there were some way to be sure that we could get a package to him."

Maria, her faith reassured, said, "We will pray, and the Lord will make a way."

The news about the packages was a disappointment, but it could not dampen their delight at having heard from Reinhold. Their hopes for his return were for the moment raised high. However, the abundance of the black censoring struck a note of concern in Maria's heart. *There are things we do not know, things which are being concealed from us. If his captors are so eager to hide information from us, what are they doing to my son? Are they giving him enough food? Are they beating him? Strengthen my son, O Lord. I do not want to lose him now.*

The return to a normal life came slowly for the Germans. The people were attempting to recover politically and economically, as well as physically and spiritually. With help from the Americans, services were slowly restored and many Germans were busy repairing and rebuilding their bomb-gutted cities. George Ziefle's experience as a salesman and as an ambulance driver didn't conform to the need of the moment for skilled journeymen and laborers. Nonetheless, George kept himself occupied as he and Kurt, somewhat hampered by his slow-healing arm, repaired their house and helped many neighbors to clean up and fix their property.

Nearly a year-and-a-half after the war had ended, George finally found a job as a chauffeur with the health department. Not only could the family profit from the income but George now enjoyed the satisfaction of providing for his family's needs.

Even before George found employment, Kurt had acquired an apprenticeship in Heilbronn at the Bär photography studio. He found the trade much to his liking and excelled in the field.

Ruth had resumed her studies in chemistry. She was looking forward to soon working as a laboratory assistant in the Vogelman chemical firm.

Helmut began first grade at the Bauschool in Sontheim. Even pencils and paper were in short supply, so the students practiced their writing skills on small blackboards which they carried to class each day. Despite the difficulties, he attacked the adventure of learning with relish.

Reinhold had now been a prisoner for over a year. He had been able to send one more letter to his family, informing of his internment in a camp in Poland. The profusion of black ink across the lines of the letter increased his family's suspicions that things were not pleasant for him. They longed to be able to see him, or at least send him something that would cheer him.

The opportunity finally came during that summer of 1946. With delight, Maria received a letter informing the family that a package from the United States had arrived for them. They could claim it at the relief center in Neckargartach, a northwest suburb. "It must be from my sister Emma, in New York," Maria concluded.

Without delay, Maria, with Ruth and Helmut, hurried off to claim their package. They took along the old baby carriage in which to carry the package, in case it was heavy. Streetcar service had been partially restored, so they were able to ride most of the distance.

Upon arriving at the relief center and receiving the package, they were glad to have brought the cumbersome carriage. The package was not only heavy, but bulky. It was addressed from Emma and her husband, Reinhold Lieb. They hurried home with their prize to open it with the rest of the family.

By the time they arrived, Kurt and George were both home from work. Excitedly they began to open the box, which in itself was no small task; the package had been well sealed and each item inside was wrapped and tightly packed. It was a glorious gift; candies, chocolate bars, chewing gum and cans of cheese and sausage left them staring wide-eyed. Maria handed each person a small sample of chocolate. They accompanied their eating with enthusiastic "M-m-m's" and "Ah-h-h's."

As they reveled in their new-found treasure, Maria suggested, "Let's save the best items and send them to Reinhold. I have a feeling that he's going through difficult times and needs these things much more than we do."

"But how will we send it if the other two packages never reached him?" George questioned.

"I have been thinking about that," Maria replied, "and I may have a solution. Reinhold said that a prisoner named Ochs from Karlsruhe did receive some packages. Since Karlsruhe is nearby, why don't we have his family send the gift for us?"

"That, Mama, is a wonderful idea!" George replied with admiration. "But who will go to Karlsruhe? Kurt and I can't get away from our jobs."

"I'll go!" offered Ruth. So the next morning, with a carefully wrapped package in her arms, she boarded the train for Karlsruhe and contacted the Ochs family, who were very willing to help.

The Ziefles had no idea how sorely needed the package was. For Reinhold, each day was lived in the shadow of death. Following capture, his unit was kept in Germany for a few weeks in order to dismantle a factory for the Russians. Once that task was completed, the prisoners were put into railroad freight cars and transported for eight horrible days through upper Silesia. The men were not allowed to leave the cars once, and were given only one cup of wheat to eat each day. Their destination: a labor camp in Jafworzno, Poland.

In Jafworzno, the prisoners were forced to work in a coal mine under Polish supervision. Receiving only minimal food rations, the men worked ten hours a day. If a prisoner stopped for only a moment to relax, a Polish guard would beat him until he returned to work. The strain began reaping its grim harvest. Having exhausted every ounce of their strength, at the end of their shift many men would sit down in the mine car, fall asleep and die. Over half of the 1,000 SS prisoners died in the first few months, so prisoners from the general army, the Wehrmacht, were shipped in to replace them.

Reinhold hung on weakly to his long-nurtured faith and managed to survive as, one by one, his comrades collapsed. One prisoner, unable to cope any longer, grabbed a guard's rifle and shot the soldier. Then he turned the gun on himself. In order to stay alive, Reinhold volunteered to perform extra duties in exchange for a larger food ration. But there was never enough to eat. One day while working near the main entrance of the mine, he noticed some oatmeal and rice in a garbage can. Quickly he scooped the food into his hands, but not before being spotted by a guard. The guard threw him on the ground. With several other booted soldiers, he walked over Reinhold until he was bruised and bloodied.

A few of the guards were kind; some even shared their meager lunches with the prisoners, but they were exceptions. Reinhold often tried to take short rests from his work, risking the beating if he were caught. It was better to rest and be bruised than to die of exhaustion.

The eldest Ziefle son came nearest to despair just before his twenty-first birthday, June 22, 1946. He had been able to hide a small piece of bread and a teaspoon of sugar from his regular rations and extra work. This would be his special birthday menu. But the day before his birthday, his treasure was stolen by another prisoner.

As long as Reinhold's sporadic letters arrived, the Ziefles knew he was alive and they remained hopeful of his eventual return. Next door, the Fischer's son, Karl, had already returned from the war, but he had become a different kind of prisoner—leukemia was carrying out its death sentence in his body. His mother, who had scoffed at Maria's trust in an unseen God, remained adamant against religious faith.

As Karl lay wasting away at the Weissenhof hospital, Maria approached the woman about her son. "How is Karl doing now?" she asked.

"Oh, he hasn't been feeling too good, Frau Ziefle—but don't worry he'll be better soon."

"But he has leukemia; he's terminally—"

"Don't be pessimistic! Karl is too young to die of a disease like that. He's strong. I'm sure he'll recover."

"I wish I could be so optimistic. I'm concerned, though, that he's not ready to die."

Frau Fischer eyed Maria suspiciously. "What do you mean by that?"

"I don't think he's made his peace with God."

The woman's face flushed with anger as she glared at Maria. "Don't you dare brainwash my son with your religion. You and your husband had better keep your Jesus talk away from him!" She stormed away.

Lord, take away her blindness, Maria prayed. *Karl is losing the life in his body and soul, and she refuses to see the truth.*

In the evening, Maria told the family about her encounter with Frau Fischer. The prayers of their Dämmerstündle that evening were not only for their imprisoned brother, but also for the Fischer family's imprisoned souls.

Undaunted, Maria, took Helmut with her to the hospital to visit Karl. His mother was at his bedside; she greeted the visitors warily, indicating with her cold response that they were not to bring up spiritual matters. The Ziefles could only hope and pray for an eventual breakthrough.

Only a few more weeks passed and Frau Fischer came to the Ziefles' house, weeping and shaking. "Frau Ziefle," she moaned, "Karl is dead." Suddenly she collapsed on Maria's shoulder, wailing loudly, "Why couldn't I do it? Why couldn't I do it?"

Maria led the distraught woman to the sofa and sat down next to her, holding her as she wept. "Tell me—what couldn't you do?" she finally asked when the woman began to quiet down.

Frau Fischer could hardly speak. "Karl was breathing his last, and he said, 'Mother, please pray with me.' I just stood and looked at him; I couldn't do it—not even the Lord's Prayer! Karl stared at me, and his eyes grew larger and larger, and—and then he died!" She broke again into weeping.

She looked at Maria, her face tear-streaked. "I knelt by my son's bed and told God to take control of my life—that I was sorry for all my rebellion." She looked into Maria's eyes. "Can God take me—after all that I've said against Him?"

Maria smiled. "Frau, we have God's promise." She put her arms around the woman and held her tightly. "Let's pray together," she suggested. The two women knelt before the bench of the old pump organ and rejoiced together in the Almighty's mercy. For Maria, the suffering and humiliation of the last years seemed a small price to pay for this moment. *Lord, if only this had happened before Karl passed away*, she thought.

But this was not the only fruit of their sufferings. A few months later, as the family ate supper in the light of the glowing wood fire, a knock at the door drew their attention. George went to see who it was. He pulled the door open and stared. "Otto! Come in! Where have you been all these years?"

The baker's former assistant followed George up into

the dining room and began to tell his story. "I was in the Wehrmacht and was captured in Russia. While I was in prison, I had much time to think—and I thought often about this moment." He looked down at the floor and shuffled his feet. "Herr Ziefle—do you still have the Bible I returned to you?" The Ziefles looked at him with surprise. "I have come back to God. I'll never desert Him or my Bible again."

Elated, George exclaimed, "Otto, you have come home in more than one way!" The whole family joined in the rejoicing. When they were seated again and listening to Otto recount his experiences in Russia, George turned to the bookcase and retrieved the Bible that Otto once had owned. Silently he handed it to the young man.

Otto snatched the book and clutched it to his chest. With tears on his face he whispered, "Lord, forgive me; your Word and I can never be separated again."

Otto was dismayed at the news that Reinhold was imprisoned in Poland. He knew how difficult life was in the east. The Ziefles, however, did not allow his comments to cause despair. Instead, they recaptured the happy moments of the past by holding a Dämmerstündle again with Otto.

Postwar reconstruction was now rapidly gaining momentum. Inner turmoil was subsiding as the Poles and other East Europeans had been returned to their countries and as German soldiers came home from Allied prison camps to reestablish their family lives.

The economy, however, was still staggering from the blows of military defeat. Millions of Germans from the eastern half had fled to West Germany; population patterns were thus thrown far out of balance. In the slowly-recovering economy, jobs for these homeless people were still nonexistent. This created friction between the Germans and the new settlers. The widening rift between the Western Allies and Russia and resulting division of Germany further added to the internal pressure.

In 1948, the Deutsche Mark was instituted to provide a stable currency. Every German citizen was given 60 Deutsche Marks as a start, and old Reichsmarks were exchanged at a rate of 10 RM to 1 DM. With the establishment of the new money system, practically overnight the stores began displaying consumer goods such as bicycles and watches which had been virtually unavailable for years. Even candy was available again.

With the new free market system and the infusion of money through the Marshall Plan, the economic recovery accelerated quickly. Soon materialism was gaining momentum. The people were frequenting their houses of worship less and less as the siren songs of prosperity and pleasure beckoned more and more loudly.

George and Maria and their children were not to be enticed. They had determined their faith in God in earlier times of prosperity; and during the years of distress, He proved himself to them all the more. They had seen the fleeting rewards of men who sought for temporal glory and gratification. They had seen the hate and the cruel pride. And at the end, they had seen the bleak humiliation that comes upon men who live for self. The Ziefles were not rich, but they were deeply satisfied. They still felt the deep anguish of the absence of their firstborn, but they were assured of the eternal joy that was set before them. They would continue in faith.

The few letters from their son continued to be heavily censored. The handwriting looked increasingly unsteady. This was cause for concern, and they always directed their anxieties to the One who understood the situation in its entirety.

It was now 1950. Almost five years had passed since Reinhold's capture. Maria casually reached into the brown mailbox and retrieved its contents. There was one envelope; it was from the German government. Curious, she tore it open and removed the letter. The notice was brief; Reinhold would arrive by train at Heilbronn in about a week.

Quivering with excitement, Maria wept as she stood outside her house. She could hardly wait for her husband and children to come home so she could tell them the news. The distress of the war had aged her beyond her 52 years; now she felt a fresh torrent of vigor within her. Her hopes had not been in vain. *God, protect him for just a few more days. Don't let anything happen to him before he comes home!*

The Ziefles prepared frantically for the homecoming. Kurt and Reinhold's room was specially cleaned and decorated. Maria baked and cooked his favorite foods. Ruth made a garland of greenery and spring flowers and hung it over the front door. Helmut, who had just turned eleven, printed a sign, "Herzlich Willkommen,"[14] and Kurt hung it above the garland. The celebration would be worthy of the Chancellor.

·

The hard wooden bench had no effect as the rhythmic click and sway of the train car lulled Reinhold to sleep. He had tried hard to recall the faces of his parents and siblings, but the five-year ordeal had blurred his memory. As his eyes closed and his head drooped, though, his subconscious replayed razor-sharp images in his mind: Mama's soft eyes, Papa's snappy wit, Kurt's bubbling energy, Ruth's poised consistency, Helmut's curiosity.

An occasional loud voice would wake him with a start— the dreaded midnight roll calls still had their effect. Assuring himself that Jafworzno was 500 miles behind him, he drifted off to sleep again.

Normal sleep patterns and a good diet would soon restore his puffy, sallow complexion, but food and rest would not heal a mind scarred by years of constant abuse and humiliation. Even Reinhold's heart, conditioned to love

---

14. "Warm Welcome."

and forgive, was plagued with the whispering taunts of revenge and resentment. The injustice of his ordeal was horribly conspicuous; he had been imprisoned and tortured as a proponent of the very regime he despised. But he was determined not to succumb to such temptation. He was the beneficiary of divine mercy; he desired the same favor for those who had despised him.

As the week wore on, the Ziefle family grew jittery with anticipation. Whenever they heard a train whistle sound in the distance, they would inwardly brace themselves for the possibility of Reinhold's appearance at their doorstep. They faithfully performed their daily duties, but their minds were virtually fixed on Reinhold's return. Each night they climbed into bed disappointed.

It was afternoon as the train slowly moved away from the Stuttgart station. Reinhold dejectedly shuffled down the aisle toward an empty seat. He slumped into the seat and looked out the window with an aimless stare. His satchel had been stolen. He had left the train to find a gift for Helmut; he would purchase it with the money he had received on his release. When he had returned to his seat the small bag was gone and someone else had taken the obviously unoccupied seat.

The contents of the satchel, though insignificant to most people, were all that Reinhold possessed after his long imprisonment. Though he would be in Heilbronn in less than two hours, he momentarily felt as if there was hardly anything left to live for. All that remained were the clothes he was wearing. He suddenly noticed how pathetic they actually looked in comparison to the other passengers' clothing. It was humiliating. He did not want to be seen this way on the streets of Sontheim. He would stay at the Heilbronn station until the sun had gone down; then he would walk home. It was Tuesday, April 25.

Kurt, who had been reading a book, stood up to stretch.

He walked to the living-room window and looked out on the street. All was quiet. The street always appeared desolate in the twilight. Kurt returned to his chair and resumed reading.

The doorbell rang. Kurt casually laid the book aside and approached the stairway. He looked out the window at the head of the stairs. He jumped as if hit by a jolt of electricity.

"Reinhold! It is Reinhold!" he screamed as he ran back to the living room to inform the other family members. "He's here! It's him!"

The others sat for a few moments as if paralyzed. The event they had been preparing for now seemed to be almost imaginary. Dazed, they rose to their feet and approached the stairway.

Realizing his thoughtlessness, Kurt blurted, "Oh, I must go and unlock the door!" He dashed down the steps.

In a few seconds, Kurt and Reinhold, arm in arm, were ascending the stairs toward their family. Helmut gazed at the brother he could barely remember. Reinhold looked closely at the eleven-year-old and exclaimed, "Helmut, you are so big!"

The others stared dumbly as Reinhold climbed the steps. Waves of relief and ecstasy poured over them. Finally Helmut ran to him. The others surrounded him with their arms as he came to the top of the stairs. They huddled together silently. Somehow Maria was able to have the best position from which to hold him tightly. He bent over and kissed her; the tears on their faces mingled in joy.

Seven years had passed since the family had been parted! Now they were all together—alive. The ecstasy of triumph surged through Maria's soul. She, with her God, had prevailed. Not even the godless Reich had been able to destroy her and her family.

Some trust in chariots, and some in horses: but we will remember the name of the Lord our God. They are brought down and fallen: but we are risen, and stand upright. (Ps. 20:7, 8, KJV)

EPILOGUE

On October, 22, 1956, George and Maria Ziefle, with seventeen-year-old Helmut, arrived in the United States as immigrants. Unable at their ages (both were approaching 60) to acquire a new language, the couple never gained U.S. citizenship. Helmut, however, became a citizen in 1965, at the age of 26. One year later, George and Maria returned to their native country and resettled in Neckarsulm.

Reinhold is married and lives in Neckargartach, a suburb of Heilbronn. He is employed at the NSU factory in Neckarsulm.

Ruth now lives in Neckarsulm and is the wife of an engineer.

Kurt eventually emigrated to the United States and operates a large dairy farm in upstate New York.

Helmut is a professor of German at Wheaton College, Wheaton, IL.

Maria Ziefle finally claimed her citizenship in the Eternal Kingdom on May 17, 1970, at the age of 71. Her greatest triumph is her heritage of godly children.